Prais

My Separate Wc

In this beautiful and compelling book, we see a daughter profoundly marked by her parents' lives, from her mother's escape from the Nazis to the secret she felt obliged to keep about her father. Bracketed by her parents' funerals, these two stories take us from the Netherlands to Surinam to Washington D.C., Indiana, Texas, and beyond, reminding us of the power of family and the healing properties of honesty.

—**Lisa Moses Leff,** professor of European and Jewish history at American University and author of The *Archive Thief: the Man Who Salvaged French Jewish History in the Wake of the Holocaust*, awarded the 2016 Sami Rohr Prize for Jewish Literature

My Separate Worlds

Daughter of the Holocaust and Evangelical Christianity

&

The Doll

Ingrid Alpern

An excerpt from this book has been previously published in slightly different form in *Bethesda Magazine.*

Table of Contents

In honor of Sally Noach whose courageous and unquestioning resistance against the Vichy Regime and the Nazis saved the lives of my grandmother, my mother, and my mother's younger sister.

My Separate Worlds

Daughter of the Holocaust and Evangelical Christianity

Meeting my Father
Again After
Nineteen Years

1.

Father, I'm almost home.
Raspberry seeds stick between my teeth
and snapdragons open to my pinch
as if I'm still exploring beneath your white porch.

The coursing river was your church.
You baptized me among the dragonflies.

But now
silver threads of Hebrew embroider my borders.
The cut leaf smell of Sukkot fills my nose.
And I bring onion studded rolls.

Where will I meet you?

2.

Mother, the ghost of a girl possesses me.
She has blunt cut hair drawn back
with a barrette.

She runs from dragonflies on a riverbank
while her father fishes.
She keeps lizards and turtles
he gives her.

She died, beating on the door
that you shut.
By possessing me,
she hopes to grow up.

3.
Aunt Lippy, nostalgia as thick as the scent of lavender
envelopes me with the tea's steam.
This pink-edged cup is a flower
from your garden beside the white porch
where a violet hid against damp dirt
and my first green lizard darted.
You sit beside me reading your verses.
I learn where my poems come from.

You have taught me to force blossoms:
yellow flowers splashed
on the somber strokes of forsythia branches.

Prologue

AFTER MOST FUNERALS I'VE ATTENDED, PEOPLE GO BACK TO THE home of the mourning family carrying salads, smoked fish, corned beef, kugels, bagels, rye bread, and coffee cakes. In the kitchen, dining room, family room, and living room, throngs of people sit or stand—and eat.

But our family drove straight from my mother's graveside to a Panera where we gathered around a table in a deserted corner without food or drink. Me, my brother and his wife, my husband, our two children, and my cousin. We took off our coats, sat down, and talked about The Secret.

We had flown into Dallas from Maryland and Massachusetts, or, in my brother's case, driven up from South Texas, to comfort my mother in her last days and then to comfort ourselves and each other, just as we had when Dad died a year and a half earlier. After Dad's private burial, we held a memorial service for family and friends, and we provided the food laden platters. For my mother, with no other place available, we were forced to hold the memorial service in the chapel of the retirement community the evening before her private burial. Not a Jewish thing to do, the rabbi's secretary informed us when she said the rabbi would only officiate at the graveside.

But this timing had allowed us to follow our unspoken compulsion. While leaving the graveside, my brother suggested we meet for coffee before we headed back out to the airport or down to the Gulf Coast.

"Follow my car," he said. "We'll find a place."

And once in that Panera, my brother, our cousin, my husband and I dove straight into the subject we had never discussed openly at a family gathering—as if we'd always known The Secret would be the agenda moments after we laid my mother in the ground.

My husband recounted the time before our engagement when I'd asked him to walk with me outside my aunt's house where the family was gathered during *shiva*, the seven days of mourning, for my grandmother. We'd been dating long enough to know we would be together. Once out of the house, I said to him, "I have to tell you something terrible about myself."

Our cousin wanted to know what my parents had said to me and how I felt about it. My brother told us he didn't know until he was fourteen years old, when our mother's older sister let something drop in the middle of a conversation and my brother's whole perception of his family changed. Our cousin reminded us that Tante Sienie, my mother, acted out of love for her family, no matter how controlling she sometimes seemed. I explained the social stigma in the 1950's, my mother's fears after the escape, and her complete lack of appreciation of cultural differences in the

United States. Our son and daughter, barely adults, sat and listened, along with my brother's wife.

What I still wanted was the catharsis I had been denied, the catharsis my mother felt every time she talked about her escape from the Nazis.

Part One

1

THE TRIP TO CRAWFORDSVILLE, INDIANA. MY FATHER'S GIFT TO ME at age four. I have carried it with me. An amulet. A compass.

We started from Virginia. My father drove. I sat beside him, arm out the window, hand cupped, fingers spread, catching the wind. White clouds billowed in light blue sky and sunshine. Just the two of us in that dusty, gray car. My father sang a lot.

I'd never heard the songs he sang anywhere else. And there was an anywhere else, already. I lived with my aunt and uncle and cousin and grandmother. My Dutch family, my mother's family. My mother and I had shown up on the doorstep of their apartment in Arlington, Virginia when I was two. It seemed like we'd always lived there with Tante Sonja, Uncle Rob, Lenny, and my grandmother, Moms.

That apartment became my world, the front stoop where Moms often sat while Lenny and I played, the woods in back, the narrow kitchen where Moms cut us pieces of butter for a snack while she cooked, the aluminum table in the living-dining room where Lenny and I drank *slappe thee* (weak tea, a half inch of tea in a glass of milk) and ate slabs of gouda on thick dark bread for breakfast.

My cousin Lenny was my partner in this world. Lenny and I in our corduroy overalls. Lenny was born in Paramaribo, Surinam a year before my birth in the District of Columbia. I loved the sing song sound of that name, Paramaribo. Lenny and I were best friends. We shared his tricycle, carried cap guns, shouted, "Hands up!" at other kids in the apartments who shouted "Hands up!" back at us, stomped the caps on the sidewalk for the bang and the burnt gunpowder smell, pursued the bell on the ice cream man's truck with dimes for fudgesicles and creamsicles, watched *The Lone Ranger* and *Howdy Doody* and kissed Howdy's face on the screen. We also got each other out of trouble.

Behind the apartment, a stream ran through a grassy field into the woods beyond. About two feet wide and several inches deep, it wasn't much of a stream. I liked to stare through the clear water at the rocks and pebbles on the bottom. One day I decided to follow that stream to its source.

Walking along the bank was not part of my plan. I needed to be in that stream. I stepped in with my shoes on. They were leather shoes, red leather, shoes that are "good for your feet," as my mother had said.

The cool water lapped at my ankles as the leather soles carried me over the rough stones and pebbles. Near the woods, the stones and pebbles disappeared, leaving mud. I pushed my heels against the slushy stream bottom, but instead of moving forward, I sank ankle deep.

"Lenny!" I shouted. "Lenny! Lenny!" From somewhere on the other side of the apartments, he came running.

"What's wrong?" he yelled.

"I'm stuck," I yelled back.

"Boy, you are," he agreed when he saw my feet.

"Go find Moms. She'll get me out."

Our grandmother knew how to do anything.

Moms was shorter than the other grownups in our family but more powerful. You could tell by looking at her, the way she stood, her back straight and her head high. And when she wanted us to do something, the glare in her green eyes made us do it.

The afternoon I was stuck, Moms strode through the field with Lenny, dressed as we usually saw her, in a flared, calf-length skirt, blouse buttoned to the collar, cardigan sweater, and her "sensible shoes," brown tie shoes with a wide, slightly raised heel, not her dressy high heels.

When she reached me, Moms grabbed my waist, pulled a few times, and I was free. She looked at my shoes.

"Ingridtje! (The *tje*, a Dutch endearment that signaled no matter what she said next I would know she loved me) Your shoes you wore? In the mud!?"

I kept my eyes on my shoes.

"Do you know how much these shoes cost? They'll never be the same, and I have to clean them. You have a nice walk and give me all this vur-r-rk. It will serve you right if I can't get out all the mud."

A few weeks later, it was Lenny's turn to be saved.

"Ingrid! Help! Ingrid! Come quick!" The street dead ended in woods that stretched as far back as we could see from the concrete curb. Lenny's voice came from those trees. I ran toward them.

"I'm coming!" I yelled. "Where are you?"

"Up in a tree," he yelled back.

I craned my neck and spotted him part way up one of the biggest trees right at the end of the street.

"What's the matter?" I yelled up to him.

"I can't get down. Get Moms."

I turned around and ran to the apartment. Moms stood in the kitchen, knife in hand, about to cut into a loaf of brown bread to make our sandwiches for lunch.

"Moms! Moms!" I shouted. "Lenny's stuck in a tree. He needs you." She put down the knife and followed me.

"Lennitje, how did you get up there!?" Her tone was one of dismay, not amazement. "Well, if you got up, you can get down."

"But, Moms," Lenny said. "I'm scared."

"Don't vuhr-r-y. I'll holp you."

"Put your right foot on the branch right below it," she said. "You can reach it. Ya. That's the one. Ya! Now the left foot there, on the branch underneath." And in that manner, Moms talked him down.

When Lenny reached the part of the trunk where there were no branches, Moms reached up and grabbed the seat of Lenny's pants.

"Come," she said. He let himself down into her arms, and she lowered him to the ground.

"You did it!" Moms clapped, and I joined her.

"So," Moms said, "let's eat lunch."

MOMS WAS OUR HERO, protector, deliverer. And though we didn't know it then, one day we would both revere her, measure ourselves by her. We would come to know it was Moms' savvy, risk taking, and courage that got us out of Europe during The War, that earned money selling her secret hoard of leather shoes to a German soldier, that found *passeurs* to sneak us past the Nazis from The Hague to Antwerp and into unoccupied France, that secured transit visas through Spain and Portugal and places on the ship to Surinam. All of this, right after her husband died.

"Us," because if my grandmother hadn't saved our parents, we wouldn't exist. "Us," because of the incredible, potent, overarching identification we have with their escape, pain, loss, fear, and anguish. Years later, when I was in college, Uncle Rob told me that before he and Tante Sonja left The Hague—months before Moms left with my mother and her younger sister, Tante Nannie—they went to say goodbye to his parents. Then barely twenty years old, Uncle Rob looked back at his parents' house as he and Tante Sonja walked away. He knew he'd never see them again. Moms offered to pay his parents' way with the *passeurs*. His parents answered, "Emma, why are you leaving home?"

But when I lived with Lenny, when he and I were between the ages of one and five, we were just beginning to learn about these things. I knew that my family was Dutch. That before The War they had lived in a beautiful house someplace far away called the Netherlands. That The War was something terrible they had to escape. That my mother was sometimes angry and afraid because she'd had to leave home on her eighteenth birthday, July 14, 1942.

IN GOOD WEATHER, we made trips on the weekends to Uncle Rob's favorite place, Hains Point in Washington, D.C. Hains Point meant sunshine, white winged sailboats on blue water, green grass where Lenny and I ran round and round our yellow and white striped blanket with its frayed satin border where the grownups sat and unpacked food from crumpled paper grocery bags: sandwiches of heavy dark bread in the uneven slices my grandmother cut from the shiny-crusted loaf, thick pieces of gouda or sometimes *wurst*, and always half-done pickles, apples, oranges, and cookies.

One Sunday, we headed for the wharf after our picnic. Uncle Rob drove with the windows down. The afternoon sun blazed through the back window, and heat rose around me where Lenny and I sat on the back seat with Moms.

I was groggy when we piled out of the car into the gravel parking lot, but Tante Sonja waved us over to one of the booths.

"Come quick!" she said.

I motioned Lenny to follow and ran toward Tante Sonja. Lenny and I flung ourselves against the rough wooden counter and peered over in the direction Tante Sonja pointed. Before us stood a man wrapped in a blood-streaked white apron, and behind him, a wall of wire cages filled with chickens. The man opened the latch to one of the cages, grabbed a chicken, carried it to a table, and picked up a cleaver. With one quick motion, the man chopped off the chicken's head and dropped the chicken to the ground. The headless chicken ran in circles on the straw covered dirt.

"It's still moving!" Lenny shouted. "What makes it do that!?" But before we got an answer, Uncle Rob called out,

"Yoo hoo, Lennitje, Ingrid, Sonja! Over here."

I pushed off from the side of the chicken man's booth and raced toward Uncle Rob, Lenny right beside me. Uncle Rob stood at a booth where Moms was talking with the man behind the counter. On tiptoes, Lenny and I stretched over the counter's edge. The man was standing beside a barrel of water.

"I want a fresh one," Moms said in the tone she used for warning us not to do something.

He stuck his arm deep into the barrel and pulled out a long fish.

"Do you have something bigger?"

He stuck his arm deeper.

"How about this one?" He held up a long, dark fish. Its tail flapped against the man's hairy arm.

"Ya. That's good," Moms said. "I'll take it. And some vater." She handed him a bucket I hadn't noticed her carrying.

The fish swam in our bathtub that night. Lenny and I pressed our pajama covered bellies against the side of the tub and laughed when we saw the shiny, dark fish slip through the water in that white porcelain bathtub where we usually took baths. Moms was going to make *gefilte* fish—fish balls the grownups liked.

EVERY EVENING WE gathered at the aluminum table in the one big room outside the kitchen, Lenny and I, Tante Sonja, Uncle Rob, Moms, and my mother, when she wasn't at work. During dinner, the grownups spoke Dutch to each other and to Lenny and me. We answered in English. They spoke loudly, often all at once, waving their arms in the air through layers of conversation that rose and hovered protectively above the table like the steam from their teacups.

Every night when dinner ended, I turned to Uncle Rob.

"Let me touch the ceiling," I begged. He picked me up and raised me high above his head, then carried me around the room, teaching me Dutch words. "Tah-hfel," he said, pointing to the table. "Lah-hmp," pointing at the lamp. Every night, before Tante Sonja trotted me off to the bedroom to get into my pajamas, Uncle Rob said to me in Dutch, "Goodnight, darling child. Sleep well." I grabbed around his neck with a hug before he put me down.

Often it was Moms or Tante Sonja who leaned over my crib (the only bed we had for me to sleep in) to kiss me goodnight. If she was there, it was my mother.

One night, my mother had already covered me, kissed me goodnight, and left the room. But I wanted her back. I wanted to play. I lay on my back and kicked the covers high.   "Mommy! Mommy!" I sang. "My covers are off. I need you."

She came in and laughed.

"Little r-r-rahscal." She smiled and covered me. "Now, sleep well, *poppetje*."

I was her dolly. I giggled and kicked the covers again.

"Oh, Ingrid, *poppetje*." She covered me again. I kicked.

"Heh. Don't act so strange! I can't anymore. I'm so tired, *poppetje*, and I want you to make it easy for me."

Something in her voice made me sad. And, then, out of nowhere, my mother blurted, "The Nazis killed my father. Those rotten Nazis."

Was this a return to being a child herself when being a parent was too difficult?

I would hear her repeat this many times.

IN THE MIDST OF THIS burgeoning history, my father gave me Crawfordsville. He showed me a whole world my Dutch family couldn't.

By then, he was already coming to take me places on the weekends. He took me to the Lincoln Memorial. I liked that big statue of Lincoln sitting way up there. He took me to a merry-go-round in a park with lots of trees. After the ticket man let me through the fence, I ran for a horse that went up and down. My father helped me mount, then stood and waved as I galloped by. He took me to the circus where we rode the Ferris wheel together.

So when my father took me to Crawfordsville, he was my Daddy who took me to places I liked.

He picked me up from the apartment in Arlington. Before Tante Sonja opened the door for him, she kneeled beside me and held me in the embrace which kept me safe every morning and every night. My cheek pressed against her soft white blouse.

"Goodbye, dear darling," she said to me in Dutch. "Have lots of fun." She looked into my eyes and smiled her smile that was almost a laugh and always made me think everything was really very funny.

My father and I embarked on a trip I'd remember my whole life, remember even when I wasn't sure exactly what it was that I was remembering, remember with an intense poignancy as if I'd realized then this was my one chance to learn about his family, store what I learned, and carry it with me through my life. He shared some treasure from his childhood at every turn. He knew this was his last chance. His chance to fill me with nostalgia for a life with him, with his family. Our family. I was, in that brief trip, to learn just that once, what that phrase meant. I was four years old.

We stopped at a park—near Crawfordsville, he told me. He held my hand while we walked. He was so tall I had to lift my hand way up high. We walked in cool air over a shaded lawn and between tall trees, until we reached a tiny hill of stones cemented together. A metal cup stood on top beside a metal spout.

"This is a spring," my father said. "Water comes from underground so clean and pure you can drink it. See, here. You can pump it up." He grasped a handle on the side of the rocks and pushed it up and down until water flowed from the spout into the cup.

"Here, try it." My father offered me the cup and helped guide it to my lips. I sipped that clear cold water.

We walked deeper into the park, and he told me we'd see big birds called peacocks.

"There!" my father whispered and pointed. I turned and saw, quite near and almost as tall as me, a bird with a wide tail of shiny green, turquoise, and blue feathers. My father and I stood, both quiet, looking.

CRAWFORDSVILLE, THE HUB of my father's life. We drove along the wide streets, beside big trees, their dark green leaves glazed with dust and sunshine. We parked under one of those trees along the curb outside the house—he told me in the car—where he grew up with his three older sisters, Kanka, Mary Frances, and Lippy, with their mother who had died, and their father, my Granddaddy. Granddaddy and Aunt Kanka lived in the house now, and Aunt

Lippy was visiting from Maryland. Aunt Mary Frances was in New York City working. Aunt Kanka was a kindergarten teacher, but she didn't work in the summer. Aunt Kanka and Aunt Lippy would be the only ones home right now. Granddaddy was at work in the bank.

"Our house," he said, helping me out of the car. "Our family's house." I stood at the curb and stared. A white clapboard house, two stories, a first floor porch, and a white porch swing. I had never been in a house before.

Two women burst out of the front door, one with her hair twisted onto the top of her head and one with short curled up hair.

"Oh you're here!" said the one with the perky hair. "We could hardly bear it, all this waiting!" She flew off the porch and across the front lawn.

The one with the twisted hair followed right behind her and echoed, "Oh, Bill, you kept us in agony with all this waiting!"

The perky-haired woman approached me. She had a nice smile.

"This is our little Ingrid!" She looked down at me. "How you've grown." My father had told me my aunts had all met me when I was a baby.

"I'm your Aunt Lippy, Ingrid." She bent down and threw her arms around me. She felt new to me, but friendly. And she was my family. I put my arms around her.

The woman with the twisted up hair knelt beside me.

"I'm your Aunt Kanka," she said. She looked into my face as if to gain my permission before she offered a hug. I felt comfortable with Aunt Kanka.

AUNT KANKA SAT BESIDE me in the wide porch swing and pushed us with her feet. Aunt Lippy and my father sat in chairs beside us.

"Come on," Aunt Kanka said to me. "Let's go exploring." I followed her to the garden beside the porch. "See here," she pointed at the shortest flowers. "These are violets."

I leaned into the damp dirt smell of the garden to look at the light purple flowers with dark purple centers.

"Oh, Ingrid," Aunt Kanka whispered, "be very still. I see a lizard." I held my breath. She pointed near the ground among the leaves of a tall yellow flower. On the lowest leaf, I spotted a lizard no bigger than the leaf and bright green, like the inside of a lime. It sat for an instant and darted away.

"I have something special to show you. Come with me." Aunt Kanka and I walked to the far end of the garden and squatted.

"This is a snapdragon." She pointed at a knobby yellow flower.

"You squeeze, and it can bite you." Aunt Kanka grinned and squeezed the sides of the narrow blossom. Its mouth opened.

"Put your finger in, Ingrid. It won't hurt you." I put my finger into the mouth of that yellow flower, and Aunt Kanka let go.

"Oh! It snapped you," she said. We laughed into each other's eyes.

As Aunt Kanka took me through that garden, I felt like she had lifted the lid of a gift box to reveal layers and layers of tissue paper that begged me to peel them away and find the treasure they concealed.

WE ALL WALKED TO the bank to meet Granddaddy after work. From behind swinging wooden doors, he emerged, tall, thick set, rectangular-headed, and white-haired. "Well, this is little Ingrid," he said in a quiet voice.

We walked back to the house with Granddaddy.

My father got our suitcases from the car and carried them into the house through the front door. I followed with Aunt Lippy and Aunt Kanka over gleaming wood floors and oval rugs, past upholstered chairs, and dainty tables that held small porcelain flower baskets.

At the top of a steep staircase, Aunt Lippy led me into a room with a plump bed covered in a nubby white cotton spread, a rag rug on the wood floor, a dresser, and a bookcase filled with books.

"This will be your room, Ingrid," she said.

WE GATHERED IN THE DINING ROOM for dinner around a large, glistening, dark wood table with curved legs and lion paw feet. Flowered placemats lay at each person's place, and in the center of the table, a squat round vase of violets sat between tall, blue, unlit candles. Aunt Kanka, Aunt Lippy, my father, and Granddaddy linked hands around the table. Aunt Lippy and my father each took one of mine. Granddaddy bowed his head and said:

Lord,

Bless this food to our use

And us to thy service;

And make us ever mindful

Of the needs of others.

In Jesus' name, Amen.

Our family prayed before dinner. In Jesus' name. Our family in Crawfordsville did that. My Dutch family didn't.

AFTER MY FATHER TUCKED ME in that night, I lay under the covers of that soft bed, the white cotton spread pulled back over my feet, the bookcase standing guard beside me. I felt accepted in a strange world, a world I was told was mine—my relatives, my family's house. I was told I belonged. Though I felt safe, I knew this was just a temporary adventure in an unfamiliar place. I would go back to the world where I lived.

AT BREAKFAST, I SAT in the sun-filled kitchen between my father and Aunt Lippy at a big white, wooden table.

Aunt Kanka stood by the sink and brought food to us.

"I think Ingrid would like shredded wheat," she said.

"What is it?" I asked.

"Oh, it's good," my father said. "We'll show you."

"This is shredded wheat." Aunt Kanka placed a bowl in front of me. A rectangular piece of cereal filled it. I'd never eaten cereal.

Aunt Lippy sprinkled sugar and poured milk onto my shredded wheat. I jabbed my spoon straight down like Aunt Lippy showed me and pried off a piece.

Our family ate shredded wheat. And toast—I discovered when Aunt Kanka handed me a piece—and raspberry jam with seeds that made the toast crunchier. All new foods to me. I liked them.

My father told me that after breakfast they were taking me to a swinging bridge in a park.

"We've gone there since I was a child," he said.

Granddaddy was coming, too. It was Saturday, and the bank was closed. Aunt Kanka carried a picnic basket. I followed her out of the kitchen door to Granddaddy's car. Aunt Lippy helped me climb onto the running board along the side of the car and showed me how to push behind the back seat into a space she called the "rumble seat" where I could stand. I was lucky, she said, because I was the only one small enough to fit back there. It was my own private place in Granddaddy's car.

WE WALKED BETWEEN TALL TREES to reach the slim bridge of rope and planks that wavered high above the river. We followed a crowd onto the wooden slats. Aunt Lippy and Aunt Kanka went ahead with Granddaddy while I stepped onto the bridge with my father.

"You go first, Honeybunch," he said. "I'll be right behind you." The bridge swayed to the rhythm of the other walkers' gaits, and each plank gave way a bit under my feet. This bridge had no enclosed sides, only one rope on each side to hold onto. I could see straight down to the river, if I looked—but I couldn't. I could slip off, or the bridge might fall.

"I'm scared," I said. "It's too shaky." My father took my hand.

"There's nothing to be scared of, Honeybunch. I've got you. This bridge won't fall. It's been here since I was a boy. You'll be just fine, Honeybunch. You'll see."

At each step I took, the bridge trembled. I clung to my father's hand. It took me a long time to reach the bank on the other side. But I liked looking back at the bridge after we walked away. In the distance, it was a little swinging bridge high above the river, almost hidden in the trees.

Aunt Kanka led us to a picnic table and unpacked her basket. We had white bread sandwiches with creamy fillings Aunt Kanka called "egg salad" and "chicken salad." She also gave me round crinkly pieces of what she called "sweet pickle" and a chocolate chip cookie. After we ate, Aunt Kanka, Aunt Lippy, and Granddaddy stayed at that table, and my father took me off by ourselves to go fishing. This was his favorite river, he'd told me at breakfast. He wanted me to get to know it.

We walked along the bank in the blue-green shade of the trees. I watched the river flow. I liked the froth where the water jumped over rocks.

"Certain parts of the river are better than others for catching fish," my father said. He stopped walking. "This is my spot. I've caught some whoppers here. I used to bring them home for your grandmother to cook."

He snapped off the lid of the metal box he'd been carrying. Inside were triple-decker shelves inhabited by what looked like toy insects with long whiskers.

"These are lures." He picked one up and showed me the long red and yellow feathers that hid the surprise hook. He fastened the lure onto his line and waded into the river in his hip boots.

I set out to explore the grassy bank. There were flowers and rocks I wanted to see. But big bugs with narrow bodies and straight across wings buzzed above me. I was sure they would dive at my head.

"Daddy! Daddy!" I screamed and ran toward the river. "Daddy!"

He looked up.

"Some terrible bugs are after me." I described them.

"They're dragonflies, Honeybunch. They won't hurt you."

Back in the tall grass, I bent toward a small white flower, and the black bugs followed my head. I tried to tell myself they wouldn't hurt me, but their name only made them seem worse. I ran to the river's edge.

"Daddy, please, please, can we go? I'm scared of these big bugs."

"Just a little while longer, Honeybunch. Dragonflies can't hurt you."

I put my arms over my head, and walked to a shady place. The bugs didn't follow. I was safe. I sat on a rock and watched ants carry leaves into a hole until my father reeled in his line and headed for the bank. He hadn't caught anything.

On our way back along the river, my father pointed and knelt by a green patch between the toes of a tree.

"This is moss," he said. "Feel it."

I knelt beside him to touch the green velvet stuff, and my father whispered, "Oh, Honeybunch, look at that!"

A turtle sat on a nearby rock in the sun.

"Look!" my father whispered, "he's going to eat a fly."

The turtle raised his head, opened his mouth, and snapped it shut.

"It's a snapping turtle," my father said. "See, his mouth is pointed. You have to be careful. He can nip a bite out of you."

AT TWILIGHT WE SAT ON THE PORCH, Aunt Kanka with me on the white swing, the other grownups in chairs. Lights twinkled in the bushes.

"Fireflies, Ingrid!" Aunt Lippy sang out. "Let's catch some!" Aunt Lippy ran into the yard and cupped her hands around a floating light. Aunt Kanka and I followed her onto the lawn. My father came with a jar for us to put them in.

"We'll make a lantern," he said.

Granddaddy joined our search for the little blinking bugs.

"There's one!" Aunt Lippy pointed at the grass, and I swooped down to cup my hands around it.

"Oh, I've got one," Aunt Kanka said.

"Now, listen here," said Granddaddy. "I'll catch more than any of you can."

My father punched tiny holes into the top of the glass jar and put it by my bed for a night light. In the dark, the bugs blinked beside me.

AUNT KANKA, AUNT LIPPY, Granddaddy, my father. They made me feel as if I were the center of their world when I was there. I have a photograph of me on that trip to Crawfordsville. I'm leaning sideways against my father, my stomach jutting out, a big grin on my face, totally unabashed.

So many miracles of childhood crammed into such a short time. So many memories. Memories confirming tranquility. Memories affirming life. Memories given by my family. In their small Midwestern town. They couldn't even imagine what my mother had faced at such a young age.

Where was Crawfordsville during "The War," as my Dutch family called it in the early years? Surely sons were killed in battle. Food was rationed. Women went to work in factories.

To us that war became known as The Holocaust. The roaring monster that breathed fire into every nook and cranny throughout Europe.

Where was Crawfordsville when my mother escaped that? It hung somewhere above the Earth like a swinging bridge in a wood, in a misty place of yellow snapdragons beside white porches, fireflies lighting the bushes, a lime green lizard on a leaf, water leaping over rocks, soft velvet moss between the long toes of a tree, a snapping turtle on a rock, his head raised to catch an insect.

My father gave me a little piece of Crawfordsville to hang around my neck and clutch in my hand. It guided me past the pieces of my mother's shattered life. Later in my life, when I saw snapdragons, small green lizards, fireflies, water rushing over rocks, moss in a forest, a snapping turtle, I gravitated toward them and felt elated—and safe.

2

ON AUGUST 5, 1944, MY MOTHER SAID GOODBYE TO MY grandmother, Tante Sonja, Uncle Rob, and Tante Nannie, in Paramaribo. They'd lived in Surinam for a year and a half, since their arrival December 24, 1942 on the ship S.S. Nyassa from Lisbon, a trip arranged by the Joint Distribution Committee and the Dutch government-in-exile to take Dutch Jewish refugees to safety. That August day in 1944, after my mother hugged her family goodbye, she boarded an airplane for the short flight to Port au Spain, Trinidad. She'd never flown before. At 4:30 am the next morning, she reported back to the airport in Port au Spain to board a sea plane for Miami. My mother entered the United States on a diplomatic visa, went through customs, and boarded her third plane—from Miami to D.C. The Dutch government-in-exile had offered her a job at the Dutch embassy in Washington, D.C. She was twenty years old.

Five and a half years later, my mother and I showed up on the concrete steps of the apartment where Tante Sonja, Uncle Rob, Moms, and Lenny lived. My mother carried one big suitcase. I walked beside her. I was two.

Throughout my life, my mother poured into me as much of her childhood in The Hague, escape from the Nazis, and early years in D.C. as she could recount. These stories formed the fiber of my existence.

They have helped me imagine her the day we left my father.

She stood in the living room of the small apartment. I stood beside her.

Twenty-five-year-old Sienie with two-year-old Ingrid—and a large suitcase.

"Come, Poppetje. It's time for our bus ride." Sienie bent down to lift her tiny daughter. She pushed the suitcase through the doorway into the hall and closed the door quietly. If only they could make it onto a bus without neighbors asking about the suitcase. Outside the building, the suitcase bumped against Sienie's leg as she held Ingrid's hand and walked down the sidewalk.

The bus came just as they reached the stop. They'd made it—and without being noticed. Sienie hoisted Ingrid into the bus and struggled up with the suitcase. She put Ingrid onto a seat, plunked down beside her, and held onto the suitcase balanced in the aisle. The first step was finished. Now she could think. They had a long ride ahead of them from Mt. Rainier, Maryland, into the District, then back out on a different bus headed to Virginia.

Beside her, Ingrid looked out the window, pointed at things, and talked about them. Sienie could answer without losing the trail of her thoughts. She felt the lightness—the excitement—of her new freedom. She was coming back to herself. No more fighting about money, how much they had, and who should control it. That horrible man, Bill Tyler, who wouldn't give her the required permission to open a bank account, tell her how much money they had, or even what bank it was in. He thought he was generous giving her cash every week, an allowance just like a child.

He said his mother was happy to keep house, take care of children, and receive household money from his father. She wasn't like his mother, Sienie argued. His mother hadn't gone to college. His mother wanted to let a man take over for her. Sienie had studied at a school in The Hague for women who wanted careers, a school the equivalent of high school and college in this country. She'd agreed not to work while she raised children. She was only asking to know how much money they had and to have equal control over it.

It hadn't done any good to explain. Bill didn't understand that what satisfied his mother couldn't satisfy her. He didn't understand that she was different. She hadn't understood their differences herself. And look at her now. She'd given up her embassy job to please him. She had no career. She had nothing.

No, not nothing. She reached for Ingrid, who turned from the window, settled her head in Sienie's lap and fell asleep. She had this two-year-old child already talking in complete sentences but still so young, still almost a baby. A whole human being dependent on her, while she had nothing to give but a warm hug. No money. No job. No husband. Not after today. She would divorce him as soon as she could. The evening before, he'd given her that possibility.

Mom had always told her marriage is important. But who would want Sienie now, already twenty-five and soon to be a divorcee, a used woman. And, if anyone did want her, would he also want another man's child? The elation she'd felt upon boarding the bus twisted inside Sienie into something drab and gray.

The last time she'd felt such despair was on her first Christmas in the United States. Christmas wasn't her holiday, but that made no difference. She was working at the Dutch Embassy in Washington, D.C. and living in the Meridian Hill Hotel, a hotel for working girls in Washington. Sienie had friends from the embassy who lived in the hotel. But on Christmas day, her friends and all the other girls in the hotel had gone home to their families. She was alone in that hotel. Her family—what remained of it—Mom, Nannie, Sonja, and Rob, were in Surinam. That day, Sienie realized she had no home to go to. It was the loneliest feeling she'd ever had.

A few months later, she met Bill.

Sienie looked down at Ingrid's little head on Sienie's lap.

Find a place to meet Jewish men, Mom had written from Surinam, not long after that lonely Christmas. This would have made sense to Sienie—before. Sienie who helped prepare for *Shabbat* by tearing enough toilet paper for the whole family to use on the Sabbath, when tearing paper was forbidden work. Sienie who joined a Zionist organization as a teenager and longed to help build a Jewish state. That Sienie loved her Jewish life.

But after The War, she was afraid to be Jewish. From the moment she, Mom, and Nannie cut the yellow stars off their clothes and left The Hague, Sienie was afraid to tell anyone she was

Jewish. Reunited with Sonja and Rob in the southern part of France, Sienie, Mom, and Nannie survived in a hotel in Nice solely because of their papers the Dutch Consul in Lyon had marked *Protestant* instead of *JOOD* on the line for religion—while all around them the French police pulled Jews down the stairs in the middle of the night. Soon after she arrived in Washington, D.C., a non-Jewish friend warned, "In this country you should stay away from Jews." Sienie decided to retain her Protestant label. She never told anyone at the Dutch Embassy she was a Jew.

Bill Tyler was a Second Lieutenant in the Signal Corps, stationed near Washington, D.C. during the war. Sienie met him at a party she attended with one of her friends from the embassy. There he was in his uniform, towering above her, his six foot five to her five foot four. He was handsome, with blue eyes, brown-blonde hair, and a shy smile. He was not the kind of handsome who would never be satisfied with only one women because he believed he could always get another.

It wasn't just his blue-eyed shyness that swept her off her feet. His three sisters, Kanka, Lippy, and Mary Frances, all living and working in Washington in wartime jobs, took her in with hugs, cups of tea, and conversation, not about clothes and hairdos, but about art and ideas and family. They told her stories about their family and made her feel part of it. Theirs was a Methodist family from Crawfordsville, Indiana.

Sienie and Bill didn't have dates. They had family outings. His sisters packed baskets of food for picnics in shady, wooded parks— or at the beach, sunny and hot—so unlike the cold, overcast beach where Sienie had walked with her friends on the other side of the

Atlantic only a few years earlier. Friends from her Zionist organization.

Sitting on the warm sand with Bill and his sisters, Sienie could easily imagine being in Scheveningen with those friends, stomping along the water quickly to stay warm, hands shoved down into thick wool pockets, the spray in that gray landscape hitting her face as they discussed building a Jewish state or argued about Nietzsche. And at a herring stand on the boardwalk, tilting back her head to chew and swallow the soft boned herring she held by the tail.

Sienie never talked about her memories. Bill and his sisters knew only that she was Dutch and had left the Netherlands during the war. That she and her family had gone to Surinam. She didn't even say, "What remains of our family." She ate the sisters' sandwiches, used her tongue to ply their white bread from the roof of her mouth, and laughed with them on their blanket on the sand.

Letters arrived from Surinam, from Mom, from Uncle Rob. *Don't marry a non-Jew*, they said. *It will cause problems later. Only a Jew can understand you.* Uncle Rob, her own sister's husband, went so far as to write that even the best marriage wasn't always easy. *Couples get angry*, he wrote. *They argue. There's plenty to argue about, when you both come from the same background.*

Sienie knew better. This Bill Tyler was nice. And he was smart, Phi Beta Kappa in college. And look at his sisters, so much like her own family, so close. When they were apart, they called each other once a week. They called Bill, too, and wrote. Her mother and Rob just didn't understand. Besides, she didn't want to be Jewish. Where had it gotten her? Out in the night, walking through woods and over fields, terrified that each flicker of a firefly was a German soldier about to beam his flashlight on her. So much better to be the same religion as everyone else.

In 1946, at age twenty-two, four years after Sienie and Mom and Nannie closed the door of their house and started the escape that ended for Sienie in Washington, D.C. at the Meridian Hill Hotel for girls, Sienie married Bill Tyler and gained three sisters. She told him she was Jewish but wanted to be Methodist and baptize their children in her new religion.

Days after her marriage in Washington, Sienie and her new sisters unpacked a picnic at Turkey Run Park in Indiana at a long wooden table under the trees, and the sisters welcomed Sienie into the family with more stories.

"Now, Bill," Lippy said, "we'll have to tell Sienie about the time you were planning to catch that big fish for Daddy's birthday."

"Oh, Lippy!" Kanka laughed and slapped a hand over her mouth.

"You two are so wicked!" Mary Frances laughed, too. "Let me tell."

Bill grinned, enjoying the attention of his older sisters. "I won't tell. That's for sure."

"Well, now, brother, I'll have to tell," Lippy said. "Our sweet Sienie ought to know exactly what kind of a person she married.

"Daddy was going to have his sixtieth birthday, and every day for weeks before the date, Bill said he would catch the biggest fish he'd ever caught, so we could eat it for Daddy's birthday dinner. Well, the day of Daddy's birthday, Bill got up extra early, put on his fishing clothes, and left the house before any of us were even awake, to drive down to the river and catch that fish. At four that afternoon, he came back with a fish in his bucket. He told us he'd had the most unusual fishing experience of his life. He'd found a place in the river where Indiana salmon lived!

"It turned out that Bill had the worst fishing day of his life. He couldn't catch anything big enough to be worth keeping. But he'd promised us dinner. So he went to the fish seller in downtown Crawfordsville, and all they had was salmon from Washington State."

That day in Turkey Run Park, Sienie donned a broad canvas hat, grabbed her new fishing pole, and waded behind Bill Tyler into the swirling waters of an Indiana river. She never mentioned the Haagse Bos, the huge woods right in the middle of the city near her house in The Hague's central business district where she'd walked with her father on Sundays. She never mentioned the last time she'd waded through a river, in her shoes and layered dresses, at night in the middle of France.

She never mentioned that memories surfaced every night in her dreams and that she couldn't escape them. She just tried— everyday. She pushed them from her mind and embraced her new life. She donned the knee-high rubber boots, the canvas hat, grabbed the aluminum bucket, and fastened her lure and even a worm. Sienie who had spent afternoons during high school down the street at the Gemeentemuseum absorbing Mondrians, Sienie who felt at ease in velvet and satin, did what it took to fit in and earn her place with her chattering new sisters. Not that they fished, but if Bill wanted her to, she would. And she would eat the picnics his sisters packed. The sweet pickles, the mayonnaise-slathered white bread with slices of roast beef or ham and cheese, the fluffy pieces of cake beneath thick icing.

In the Netherlands, pickles weren't sugary and soft, or rippled. In a delicatessen at the end of her street in The Hague, the smells of garlic and vinegar rose from a wooden barrel where dark green pickles, crisp to the bite, lay in the brine, just waiting for Sienie to pay her nickel and reach in. In the Netherlands, pastries were flaky and layered or thick like the spiced cookies filled with almond paste. At home, sandwiches were made of heavy dark bread, either meat or cheese, but never both together, and never ham.

Dear God, Sienie had prayed when a farmer yelled at her, Mom, and Nannie as they walked across his fields at the Belgian border, please protect us. *I haven't been able to eat kosher food. Please forgive me. If I survive, I promise I will eat only kosher food again.*

She never did. And, married to Bill, she pushed all those thoughts from her mind. Her life was with Bill and his sisters. She was alive.

She was even willing to celebrate Christmas. And that first Christmas with Bill and her three new sisters there had been so much to celebrate. She was pregnant.

But their marriage had deteriorated into arguments, and she'd come to see their differences. And now, after barely two years of marriage, in the middle of their argument the night before, he'd reached out and struck her face with the palm of his hand—hard. She'd grabbed Ingrid and locked themselves in the bedroom. He'd never done anything like that before.

He was distraught, yelling through the bedroom door, "Sweetheart, forgive me! Please Sweetheart, I don't know what got into me."

Her silence from the locked bedroom silenced him. The side of her head ached. What kind of a man hits his wife? Only crazy or very coarse people acted that way. Unexpectedly, her decision had been made. Now she knew for sure. The arguing was over. She wanted a divorce. By the time he left for work this morning, the suitcase was packed.

Sienie patted Ingrid's soft blond hair and leaned back against her seat on the bus.

Family is everything, Mom had always told her. After The War, Sienie only had Mom, Nannie, Sonja, and Rob—and now Lenny and Ingrid. She knew Sonja and Rob would take them in. She'd build a career so she could support herself and Ingrid.

3

WHEN WE LIVED WITH TANTE SONJA AND UNCLE ROB, I DIDN'T realize that my mother left to live in Florida—until I visited her. It wasn't until I went to law school over twenty years later that I understood she went for three months to establish residency in Florida and get the divorce. I was two years old when I visited my mother. The airlines let very young children fly alone back then.

Tante Sonja took me to the steps of the airplane and introduced me to the stewardess, a blonde haired woman in a dark suit with lots of gold buttons. I was going to visit my mother in a place called Florida. She was living there now. I was dressed in my navy blue coat. I sat by the window, looking at the clouds. The stewardess came by all the time to ask if I was alright and if I needed anything. She gave me a tray with food on it.

I threw up, and the stewardess wiped off my navy blue coat. When we landed, the stewardess took me down the stairs from the plane to my mother.

"My Ingridtje," my mother said, enfolding me in her arms though I smelled like vomit.

My FIRST MORNING in her apartment, we ate our cheese and bread on a table that pulled down from the wall beneath the window.

"From this window," my mother said, "you can see a bridge that splits in two and lifts up to let boats go by. It's called a drawbridge.

"Look, Ingridtje! Quick! See?" The two of us stared out the window to watch the two sides of the bridge rise while some boats floated by and the bridge closed again.

She took me to the zoo. On the bus, she pointed to big umbrella trees. "Those are palm trees. And, see, way up there, those brown balls? Those are coconuts."

Right inside the entrance to the zoo, my mother led me to a place where I could see pools, rocks, and palm trees beyond a wire fence. Pink birds taller than I was stood beneath the trees on thin knobby-kneed legs.

"Those are flamingos," my mother said. "They're my favorite birds."

That afternoon, my mother introduced me to a man by the pool at her apartments.

"My boyfriend," she called him as we walked to the pool. "I want you to meet him." He came right up to us when we reached the pool, all tan and muscles and hairy chest, dressed only in a bathing suit. All the men I'd seen wore shirts and trousers. My mother wore a bathing suit, too. I wore shorts and a T-shirt. I didn't own a bathing suit.

The boyfriend and my mother talked and laughed. I could tell she was sharing the boyfriend with me like she shared the flamingoes. But she was laughing in a way I hadn't heard her laugh before.

The boyfriend had a name I don't remember, but he did two things to make me remember him. Before I was the slightest bit used to him, he held out his forearm and asked me to lick it.

"Lick my skin," he said. "I've been swimming in the ocean. It tastes like salt water."

I didn't want to put my tongue on a strange man's skin. I stood there and looked at my mother. She leaned back on a reclining chair beside me.

"Don't you want to taste the ocean?" the boyfriend asked.

My mother threw back her head and laughed as if it were a joke.

"Ya. Go on, Ingrid," she said.

I stuck out my tongue and wiped it against the boyfriend's hairy arm just above his wrist.

"Doesn't it taste salty?" he asked.

I nodded and looked down.

But the boyfriend wasn't finished.

"Come on." He motioned to me, "Do you want to swim?"

"No," I said. "I don't know how."

"Oh, come on," the boyfriend said. "I'll take you in."

I'd licked his hairy arm. Wasn't that enough?

My mother was laughing again, her head tilted back, her long dark hair spread on the chair behind her. The ends slipped against her shoulders. She looked at me.

"Go ahead, Ingridtje," she said. "It will be alright."

"Get on my back," the boyfriend said, "and hold on tight. I won't let anything happen to you."

The boyfriend got into the pool, and my mother helped me climb onto his massive back, slippery with lotion. The question of whether or not I wanted to embrace his slippery skin was not one I could debate.

"Hold on," he said. "You'll be O.K. I gotcha."

I spread my arms wide to clutch his shoulders, and before I could get my bearing, the body upon which I perched lunged forward, the arms and shoulders rising and falling, me along with them.

I felt as if I could slide into the water face first at any moment. But he didn't leave that to chance.

"Hold on!" he yelled and plunged under water. Water surged up my nose. Splinters entered my brain. Water gagged my throat. We surfaced in seconds. I choked and coughed and screamed and cried. Long after he'd carried me to the edge and handed me to my mother. Long after she'd sat me in a chair and wrapped me head to foot in a towel, I choked and coughed and cried.

"How could you do that to her?" my mother raged at him. "You gave her no warning! You knew she couldn't swim!"

She no longer lay on the recliner, her dark hair spread out behind her. She kneeled on the concrete, her arms tight around my towel-wrapped body. The glare in her voice was unmistakable, and I could imagine the glare in her eyes, though they were focused on the man who was still a stranger to me. It seemed as if he were a stranger to both of us now.

I TOOK SWIMMING LESSONS during the summer after first grade, and on the very first day, the teacher complained to my mother that I wouldn't put my head under water.

I looked at my mother. "You know why," I said.

She told the teacher not to push me. I'd put my head under when I was ready. In the car on the way home, my mother said, "Do you remember what that man did to you? That was awful."

I didn't put my head under water until I was fourteen.

WHEN MY MOTHER returned from Florida, I didn't know she was working for a brokerage firm as a statistician and had been taking a correspondence course at night—or that she became a stock broker on the New Stock Exchange.

I only knew that when she was around, my mother went places with us, Tante Sonja, Uncle Rob, Moms, Lenny, and me.

One time, all of us piled into Uncle Rob's car and drove into the District to Posin's, a delicatessen. Inside Posin's, Lenny and I stared through the tall glass counter at the plates of smoked fish, salads, pickles, and large round cheeses. We watched the man behind the counter in the long white apron dip his metal spoon into the containers and lift the large cheeses onto a wooden board by the sink to cut off wedges as Moms, Tante Sonja, and my mother ordered pickled herring, half done pickles, gouda, edam, and Uncle Rob's favorite Dutch cheese, *komijn kaas*, a hard yellow cheese dotted with chewy cumin seeds.

Armed with their bags, Moms, Tante Sonja, and my mother led us out to the vestibule between the outside and inner doors. Uncle Rob went to get the car.

People waited around us. Others passed in and out of the delicatessen. The grownups talked. I listened. Lenny explored the newspaper machine. He stuck his hand into the place where the change came back and pulled out a fistful of coins.

"Hey, look at this!" He extended his palm to Tante Sonja.

"You should make him give it back," a woman near us said to Tante Sonja in a bossy tone.

"She's right," another voice chimed in. "It doesn't belong to him."

From all around me, I heard voices saying, "How can she let her child do a thing like that? What kind of people are they!"

My mother looked straight at the first woman and said loud enough for everyone to hear, "Who should he give it back to?"

The voices stopped. The woman looked confused. She turned and walked away.

"Let him keep it, Sonja," my mother said in the same loud voice.

4

MY NEXT AIRPLANE RIDE WAS TO ST. LOUIS—THE TRIP TO
Crawfordsville one month behind, and my fifth birthday a few
weeks ahead.

At the St. Louis airport, the stewardess walked me down the
airplane steps to my mother who bent and hugged me there on the
vast stretch of concrete. "Ingridtje! *Lieverd*!" She said into my hair,
using a Dutch endearment.

Though only four months, it seemed like a long time since I'd
seen her. But I felt I belonged with her, like being with Tante Sonja
and Moms. I pressed myself into her hug.

A man behind her smiled at me.

"This is your new Daddy," my mother said.

"Does he live with us?"

They both laughed. He, with delight in his eyes.

"Yes, he lives with us. He's my husband, and he's your Daddy.
He loves you just like I do."

"What do I call him?" I looked at my mother.

"Daddy."

There it was. That simple. The beginning of the substitution.

We drove from the airport to my new home, "our apartment" my mother called it, as she opened the front door to reveal a little room filled with a double bed covered by a green spread. I followed her to the right, down a hallway where a small aluminum table jutted from a one person kitchen—a sink, stove, oven, and a few white metallic cabinets and drawers in a tiny alcove. At the end of the hallway, my mother showed me a bathroom and a bedroom big enough for a rollaway bed and a lamp table. This was my room.

Daddy put down my suitcase, and my mother said it was dinner time. "Go wash your hands, Ingridtje."

The three of us sat around the aluminum table beside the tiny kitchen. I immediately discovered the meat was too tough and pushed it under my other food.

"Heh, Ingrid, eat your meat," my mother said.

"It's too hard to chew."

Daddy laughed. "See that drawer over there?" He pointed to one of the kitchen drawers. "That's the candy drawer. You eat your meat all up, and I'll give you a candy bar for dessert." He opened the drawer and held up a bar in white and red wrapping.

"C'mon. Let's see what we can do here."

Daddy cut a piece of my meat, stabbed it with a fork, and held it near my closed mouth. "See this piece of meat?" he asked. "This is a knight in shining armor—a guy who works for a king and dresses up in shiny metal." This knight, Daddy explained, had ridden a long way on horseback back home to his castle. He just rode over the drawbridge above the moat, a ditch full of water that keeps bad guys out of the castle. Now, he was waiting in front of the portcullis, the gate to the castle walls. My mouth was the portcullis.

"Open the portcullis, and let me in!" the meat cried out in Daddy's voice.

My mouth sprang open to admit the knight. In a very short time, Daddy handed me that candy bar.

"You know," he said, as I bit into it. "After you're finished eating, if you can get into your pajamas, brush your teeth, and hop into bed quick as can be, I think I'll have time to tell you a story."

Daddy pulled up a chair to the side of my bed and told me a story about Elaine, a girl like me who loved her "Mummy and Daddy" but always made up reasons to go into the backyard so she could sneak away for adventures with the Mugwumps, little men who lived in hollow tree trunks in the woods behind Elaine's house. Elaine had picnics with the Mugwumps and saved them from witches.

DADDY WASN'T HOME MUCH, because he was a "resident" curing people at the hospital. But when he was home, Daddy spent time with me.

He sat on the chair by my bed, with me crouched on the bed beside him while he made a Plasticine jungle and Plasticine monkeys that stood on my lamp table. His big square hands, so clean they were shiny and transparent enough to show the blue blood vessels, molded bits of the soft clay into oval monkey heads. His strong white thumbnail precisely inscribed each monkey's grin.

He sang me songs from *The Mikado*. "Yes, sir. I performed in *The Mikado* in a men's chorus during medical school at the University of Toronto," he told me. "I grew up in Canada, a country not too far from the United States where we live." He sang me other songs, too, silly ones that made me laugh.

"Oh you mustn't stick your hand out the window," Daddy instructed me once in the car. "I've seen people in the emergency room with their arms ripped off by a passing car." Those big square hands sewed up people as carefully as they made my monkeys. I pulled in my arm, with special knowledge from Daddy. My Daddy.

But there was more to learn about my new life. Sometimes my parents sat around the table way too long after dinner, or they went off to take a nap in the afternoon. I went to my room, all alone. No Lenny to share it with. No Lenny to play Old Maid with while the grownups slept late on Sundays. No Lenny to tease me when he won until I screamed and woke them up. No Lenny. No other kids around. No place to play outside. I went to my room and learned to play alone.

OTHER SUBSTITUTIONS WERE MADE, careful substitutions. One night at the aluminum table, I was shoving some stringy meat under the roasted potatoes on my plate when my mother said, "We're a family, now. A Jewish family." She smiled at me.

"You've always been Jewish. Because you come from a Jewish mother."

"That's right," Daddy chimed in. "It's Jewish law, y' know. Only Jewish children come from a Jewish mother, see. So you're Jewish just like the rest of us. Mummy, me, my mummy and daddy, Tante

Sonja, Uncle Rob, Moms, Lenny. We're all in the same club. And it's a great club to be in." Tante Sonja, Uncle Rob, and Moms had never mentioned being Jewish.

During another dinner conversation, Daddy said when he was a kid a store hung a sign outside saying kids would get a lollipop if they came upstairs to be baptized. "All my friends and I did it every weekend. We wanted the lollipops. It didn't mean a thing to us. We thought it was great fun."

I laughed.

DADDY WAS AT THE HOSPITAL. My mother cooked dinner while the radio blared about Eisenhower for president.

"I'm for Eisenhower," I announced. A nearly five year old emulating her father back in Virginia.

"Where did you get that?" my mother asked sharply, her eyes angry.

"My father says so."

"He's for Eisenhower. We're for Stevenson, a smart, smart man. Eisenhower's no good."

MY NEW DADDY CAME with a new aunt and uncle. Daddy's sister, Aunt Julia and her husband, Uncle Joe, lived in St. Louis. Uncle Joe was doing a residency at the hospital, just like Daddy. They seemed to spend most of their time there. My mother and I spent a lot of time with Aunt Julia at her house.

One Saturday morning, in the car on the way to see Aunt Julia, my mother said, "Aunt Julia's one of the most brilliant women I've ever met. And she's one of the most interesting. She's read so many books, she can talk about almost anything. I love being with her."

So did I.

Not long after I moved to St. Louis, Aunt Julia held my fifth birthday party at her house. I'd never had a birthday party before.

"Here's the birthday girl!" Aunt Julia sang out when she opened the door for me and my parents. She grabbed me up into a bear hug.

"Come into the kitchen." Aunt Julia took my hand.

The kitchen table was covered with layers of newspaper and more lay in a pile on the table next to paste jars, colored paper, and scissors.

"We're going to make hats and decorate them," Aunt Julia explained.

The doorbell rang. Other families arrived.

While the grownups talked in the living room, the kids sat around the kitchen table where Aunt Julia helped us fold sheets of newspaper into pointed hats. She showed us how to cut shapes from construction paper and paste them onto our hats.

I smeared swabs of white paste onto my hat and pressed my colored shapes into the sticky spots.

"Is everybody finished?" asked Aunt Julia.

"Yes!" we chorused.

"Then let your hats dry and follow me."

She led us through the kitchen, out the screen door, into a rectangle of grass behind the house where Uncle Joe stood with a garden hose near a blow up wading pool.

"Step right up," he called with a grin. "Anybody have any paste to wash off?"

We surrounded Uncle Joe in our T-shirts and shorts. He sprayed off our hands, and we ran for the pool.

Aunt Julia emerged from the house with a plastic hat that she screwed onto the hose.

"Who wants to be first to wear this squirting hat?" she called.

"I do!" one boy yelled as he leaped from the wading pool. Aunt Julia strapped the hat on his head and turned on the hose. The boy ran around the yard, spouting water from the top of his head. Grownups slammed through the screen door to watch and laugh. That was my favorite part of my party.

Three other families came to that party. The fathers were all residents with Daddy and Uncle Joe. On weekends our parents went over to Aunt Julia and Uncle Joe's house to play cards. The kids and I played board games. I had playmates.

AUNT JULIA TOOK ME TO MY FIRST *Purim* festival. In the car, she explained that *Purim* is a Jewish celebration of the time, long ago, when the Jewish Queen Esther and her cousin, Mordechai, saved the Jews from a bad man named Haman. At a *Purim* festival, kids dress up like the characters in the story and eat *Hamantaschen*, cookies shaped like Haman's triangular hat.

"We're going to dress you up like Queen Esther." Her broad grin and sparkling eyes filled me with excitement.

We stopped at her house where Aunt Julia held up some white gauzy material. "These used to be curtains, but they'll make a perfect dress for a queen."

She wrapped the filmy stuff around me and tied it at my waist with a silver ribbon.

"You look bee-uu-tiful!" she exclaimed.

Aunt Julia drove us to a big gray building she called her synagogue, a place where Jews go to pray and be together, she explained. I'd never heard of a synagogue. My mother hadn't yet told me about her synagogue in The Hague. Inside, we held hands and headed down a hallway. Our footsteps echoed on the stone floor until we reached a door at the end.

"Here we are. Let's go in!"

We entered an enormous, brightly lit room crowded with adults, other kids in costumes, and tables holding trays of cookies. In the middle of the room stood a platform with steps at both ends. A man beside the platform began to speak into a microphone.

"Welcome to our annual *Purim* festival," he boomed.

The room became quiet, and people turned to look at him.

"As we do every year, we're going to have a parade so everyone can see the costumes you're wearing today. Whoever wants to join the parade line up beside me. We're about to begin!"

From all over the room costumed kids moved through the crowd, and soon a heaving, swaying line of kids wound from the platform around the edges of the room. Someone at a piano somewhere began to bang out music. Aunt Julia joined others to sing, "Oh, once there was a wicked, wicked man. And Haman was his name, Sir."

From beside Aunt Julia, I watched the line of kids climb the wooden steps. Each kid stood on the platform for a moment before descending on the other end. Aunt Julia stopped singing and looked down at me.

"Do you want to go up there?"

"Yes."

"O.K. I'll meet you when you come down."

All by myself, I joined the line. On my turn, I stood still on the platform like I'd seen the others do, so everyone in the room could see my costume. I was with Aunt Julia, and I knew I was beautiful.

Aunt Julia met me at the bottom of the steps. "Oh, Ingrid, you looked like a queen, and you didn't look the least bit scared up there in front of all those people. Let's get some *Hamantaschen*."

We joined the throngs of kids and grownups around the tables, all reaching for the big triangular cookies.

MY PARENTS AND I STAYED in St. Louis one year, then we moved to Texas. Daddy was going to do research at M.D. Anderson in Houston.

By the time we crossed the state line into Texas, I was a Jewish girl with a Jewish family—and a Democrat. My borders had been established.

5

WHEN WE DROVE TO TEXAS, WE WERE A THREESOME. IT WAS US against the world. We laughed at the grits on our plates at breakfast in the Texarkana motel restaurant, that mushy white stuff between the eggs and toast. My mother asked the waitress what it was called.

"Ich. Awful." My Dutch mother scrunched her face in disgust after the waitress left our table.

We laughed at the accents.

"Yes, sir, folks," my Canadian Daddy declared, "definitely not the Queen's English they speak around here. I could hardly understand a word that waitress said."

Part of this us-against-them attitude held an undeniable tinge of arrogance. These Texas accents sounded uneducated to my parents who valued education and were definitely educated themselves.

"In the Netherlands," my mother said, pushing the grits to the edge of her plate, "educated people speak a very good Dutch."

I rode part way from St. Louis to Houston in Daddy's old gray Oldsmobile and part way in my mother's yellow convertible. In both, I had important jobs: stuffing newspaper into cracks in the black convertible top to keep out the rain and red mud slung by the Arkansas wind, and looking for signs that we were on course—cattle grazing, piney woods, and oil derricks.

OUR THREESOME, OUR US-AGAINST-THEM laughter formed my haven. And once situated in our apartment in Houston, we initiated rituals, a matrix of safety, coziness, and fun.

Daddy's telling me Elaine and the Mugwumps bedtime stories became a nightly event. He pulled up a chair to the side of my bed and launched into another episode.

"Benny, come on now. Ingrid has to go to school tomorrow. Get out of there," my mother said to Daddy every weekday night in the middle of Elaine's adventures with the Mugwumps. Daddy always finished the story.

Every Friday night, my mother lit *Shabbat* candles for the Sabbath in two unmatched bronze candlesticks that were somehow connected with her home in The Hague. We ate steamy, onion-spiked potato kugel with our meat and vegetables. After dinner we went to the drugstore to read magazines, the treat we looked forward to all week, even discussed several times during weekday meals.

The magazine rack covered an entire wall at the drugstore. My parents stood. My mother read *Vogue* or *House Beautiful*. Daddy read *Newsweek* and flipped through *Life* and *Look*. I sat nearby on the linoleum floor beside the comic books, immersed in *Little Lulu*, in Lulu's adventures with Witch Hazel and her daughter, Little Itch, and Tubby's adventures with Sammy the tiny space man.

Besides his medical research at MD Anderson Cancer Center, Daddy taught anatomy at the dental school. My mother taught Hebrew school to make ends meet. It wasn't until several years after we moved to Houston that *Look*, *Life*, and Daddy's favorite magazine, *Commentary*, showed up in our apartment. By then, I collected one penny a week allowance until I could afford a 10 cent *Little Lulu*.

When my mother and I drove places together, I ordered the gas. "People just don't understand me when I say r-r-r-regular-r-r gas," she explained to me. "Would you please tell them what I want?"

The gas station attendant came over to my mother's side of the car and asked, "What kanda gas d'y'all wawnt, Ma'am?" I leaned as close as I could to my mother and said, "Regular gas, please."

WE LIVED IN A BIGGER APARTMENT in Houston. A living-dining room stretched from a picture window with venetian blinds at the living room end to our air conditioning unit propped in the small window at the dining room end. There, a Sears and Roebuck gray and white marbled Formica table stood on aluminum legs. A separate kitchen, two small bedrooms, and a bathroom branched off the living-dining room. Our apartment was on the first floor, in a string of two story buildings that looked like motel units, but without a pool in back— just a fenced-in concrete rectangle with swings and a teeter-totter.

That tiny playground behind our apartment was where I met the girl I invited to my birthday party. My sixth birthday occurred right after we moved to Houston, before school started. We barely knew anyone, but my mother wanted to give me a party.

"In the Netherlands, birthdays are very important," she said. "When I came to the breakfast table on my birthday, I found cards and little gifts my mother had put at my place. I always took some kind of treat to school for my friends—cookies or candies. When you get older, you invite all your friends to your house, or to a pastry shop, for pastries."

I only knew one person in Houston, a girl my age I met on the swings. My mother invited her and her mother to see a movie with us and have ice cream afterwards.

A few weeks later, I started first grade. My mother made treats for my breakfast, French toast. A typical Dutch sandwich of butter and *hagelslag*, the Dutch version of chocolate sprinkles. Or what she called a Dutch pancake, a thin pancake the size of a plate.

DADDY INSTITUTED OUR family trips to the library.

"We're going to the library today," Daddy said one Saturday as I cut into a syrup soaked corner of my French toast.

We couldn't afford to buy books, he told me, but we didn't need to. His parents couldn't afford books either, but he always had books to read. The public library was walking distance from his house. They let people take home books for free. His library had a rule that kids were required to check out one classic—a book by a really good writer the librarian would recommend—along with any other book. That way, he explained, he read all the great writers.

He and Aunt Julia lived off the public library, absorbing every bit of imaginary life into their minds. That's where those jungles complete with monkeys he molded for me out of Plasticine must have come from—and all those hours and hours of bedtime stories he made up.

"Say." Daddy looked across the table at me. "When I was about your age my favorite books were about Dr. Doolittle, a doctor who spoke animal languages. He helped them and travelled with them—even to the moon.

"Do you think you might want to check out a Dr. Doolittle book today?"

"Yes!" I couldn't wait to read it.

WE PARKED OUTSIDE THE BIG building and climbed what seemed like hundreds of stone steps through the muggy Houston air to reach the entrance. Inside, Daddy introduced me to a lady librarian. She handed me a little card labelled Houston Public Library and told me to sign my name on it.

"Do you have Dr. Doolittle books?" Daddy asked.

"We sure do. I'll show you the children's room."

She led us to a big room with shelves from ceiling to floor and a wide window with tiny frames all through it above a window seat. We followed until she tilted a book off the shelf for Daddy. He handed it to me.

Daddy showed me how to check out my book at the front desk.

As we left the library, he said, "You'll never be lonely if you have books to read."

Books became my best friends that day.

6

ON THE FIRST DAY OF CHRISTMAS VACATION IN FIRST GRADE, I WAS home alone with my mother.

"Ingridtje, I have to tell you something." Her voice was quiet, foreboding.

"The Shvantz is coming."

"Who?"

She laughed. "Oh, that's what Daddy and I call Bill Tyler. It's a Yiddish word. It means a . . . tail, a useless tail."

Bill Tyler. My father. I hadn't heard his name since Tante Sonja put me on the plane in Washington, D.C. and sent me to St. Louis to my mother and my new Daddy, sometime before my fifth birthday.

"He's coming," my mother said. "He'll be here every day for a week. Right after lunch every day, you wait by the window. When you see him, go out."

"Won't he ring the doorbell?"

"No. I wrote him not to come to the apartment. I'll tell you when to start looking out the window."

My mother had called him The Shvantz. I'd heard this word before when she'd told me about her Uncle Morris, her father's brother. "He was a *shvantz*," she'd said. "He could never make a living." Her father felt sorry for him, she'd explained. He gave Uncle Morris a job in her father's shoe store at the cash register and let Uncle Morris live with them. My mother often talked with pride about her parents' business prowess, the two movie theaters and the shoe store her father owned in The Hague before The War, and the fact that Moms ran the shoe store. Without her father's help, poor Uncle Morris couldn't support himself.

"That uncle of mine," my mother repeated the day I first heard the word. "He was a *shvantz*."

THE NEXT DAY AFTER LUNCH, I waited on a chair beside the venetian blinds of the living room window in our apartment, my neck craned sideways to look out the window, my stomach queasy. I focused on dust motes floating near the blinds. No conscious memories. No conscious feelings. My mother who always sat with me while I ate, even if she wasn't eating, didn't sit with me while I waited. She was busy in the kitchen.

A car pulled up to the curb and parked. A tall man emerged and stood by the car. I recognized him.

"He's here," I said with as little intonation as possible.

My mother emerged from the kitchen and kissed me on the cheek.

I opened the door to our apartment and closed it slowly behind me. I needed to walk across the lawn to the man my parents had turned into The Shvantz. I knew he was watching me. Me unprepared. Me barely six years old. Out there alone, crossing that lawn from my parents to him.

In Judaism, *Shabbat* begins at sundown on Friday. A time to reflect, to rest, a time out from the demands of life—a sacred day. One of the Ten Commandments: Remember the Sabbath day and keep it holy.

At sundown on Saturday, *Shabbat* ends with *Havdalah*, the transition between the sacred respite, *Shabbat*, and the mundane world of work and routine. In the *Havdalah* ceremony we accept the sacred, the venerated, the holy, along with the impure, the defiled, the profane, the ordinary, all as integral parts of our one life, integral parts of the world.

But for me, crossing that lawn between the apartment and the car, there was no *Havdalah*, just that word, *shvantz*.

When I reached the car, my father leaned down and kissed my cheek. "How are you, Honeybunch?" he asked.

That moment crystallized my dilemma. If I was nice to him, I would betray my parents.

In an instant, I chose my strategy, be nice but say as little as possible.

"I'm fine," I said softly.

THAT EVENING, I walked back across the lawn toward the apartment. I knew he was watching me. I did not know yet that in my life two worlds had been delineated.

SOON, VERY SOON, the separateness of those two worlds presented their first impact. After his visit, The Shvantz sent me a book.

My mother gave me the book, unwrapped. "This came for you from The Shvantz."

It was *A Child's Garden of Verse: The Golden Book of Poetry.* There was a garden on the cover. Elves and little children played beneath the lush foliage. I lifted the cover. On the inside page my father had written, *To Ingrid, with love, Daddy.* I wanted that book. But a malignancy rose from that inscribed page. *Daddy. Daddy.* The book couldn't enter the world where I lived with my mother and my Daddy. This inscription might taint the place where we lived, and taint me.

My parents understood the explanation I gave. I wanted the book, but the page made me feel bad. Daddy razor bladed the page out of the book. My mother signed the next page with my name Ingrid Roth, the name I used every day. Roth was Daddy's last name, our family's last name.

Together they made the book safe and brought it into the sacred, the world in which I lived with my parents.

My father sent me the only books I owned for many years. I know which books he sent, because they were all razor bladed and inoculated with my name. My parents taught me that the way to deal with something you don't want to cope with is cut out the pages and they no longer exist—not in the world you live in. For me there was no *Havdalah.*

7

WE WERE A FAMILY TUNED TO NEWS ON CAR RADIOS, HOME radios, (eventually television), and in magazines and newspapers.

"It's very important to know what's going on," my mother told me. "So you can protect yourself."

Together, my parents analyzed every detail of whatever they heard or read. They invited friends over to debate their conclusions.

And when I entered first grade, Daddy began to give me lessons.

At dinner the first night of first grade, I told Daddy what I'd told my mother that afternoon. After the teacher called roll, the principal's voice came on the loudspeaker to lead us in the Pledge of Allegiance and in a prayer she called The Lord's Prayer—clearly a Christian prayer.

"I felt awful," I told Daddy. "We had to stand up. I stood there and repeated the *Sh'ma* under my breath." Saying the holiest Jewish prayer seemed to insulate me from the atmosphere in that school room.

"That's my smart girl," he said. I glowed inside. "You did the right thing. They shouldn't be saying Christian prayers—or any prayers at all—in a public school. But there's nothing you can do except find ways, like you did, to put up with it. It's no good trying to fight this sort of thing. And there's no need to say at school that you're Jewish. Don't bring attention to it.

"There's plenty of antisemitism around. When I was a kid, the non-Jewish kids chased me on my way home from school. I came to the States after medical school—just like Uncle Joe—because Jews couldn't get residencies in `. Yes sir, I've learned about antisemitism. It's no good making a stink at your school about that prayer."

Daddy's straight forward way of discussing what bothered me always made me feel better. I felt safe in our trusting, confiding threesome.

FROM DADDY I LEARNED the bad guy of our time was Joe McCarthy, some senator up in Washington, D.C. who was ruining people's lives by calling them Communists and spies for the Soviet Union. They lost their jobs, and some were put into prison. He often went after Jews. The United States, Daddy explained, was in a "cold war" with the Soviet Union, a communist country and a dictatorship which meant one person runs the whole country instead of letting everyone vote and have a say in how the country is run. A cold war meant our countries didn't like each other, but we weren't fighting with weapons. Many people were afraid communist spies for the Soviet Union lurked all over the United States. McCarthy's way of gaining power, Daddy explained, was to use that fear. McCarthy called people he hated something other people were afraid of.

"He's a real No Good-nik. It's a crying shame what he's doing to people!"

Daddy delivered this lesson at the dinner table, a few nights after the prayer discussion. I pushed my meat around my plate while he talked.

"And listen, Ingrid," Daddy put down his fork and looked me straight in the eyes. "It's best not to talk in school about what we say here at home. I heard from some parents at your school that principal of yours is in an organization that supports Joe McCarthy. She talked to these parents about it at a school meeting, tried to get them to join."

"Did they join?" I asked.

"No! These people think Joe McCarthy is a skunk, just like we do. They were polite as can be to that principal because their kids are in her school, but they couldn't wait to get away from her."

Daddy picked up his fork, and looked over at me again.

"And never tell anyone we voted for Adlai Stevenson. We've got to watch out, see. This place is conservative as Hell. You and I know what's good for us, see?" He gave me a great big wink. I was lucky to have a smart Daddy who taught me important things and didn't treat me like a child.

I LAY, PROPPED ON MY ELBOWS, on the living room floor reading the Sunday comics. Daddy, on the couch near me, slammed his book shut. I looked up.

"Take a good look at this man, and never forget him," Daddy said. He held up the book. I saw a yellow book jacket with the black outline of a man's profile, mostly a swooping nose.

"That's Richard Nixon," Daddy said. "He's a bad, bad man. A friend of Joe McCarthy, but plenty bad all on his own. Nixon recently messed up the life of a woman in California named Helen Gehagan Douglass by calling her a Communist."

MY MOTHER ALSO OFFERED LESSONS. The first week of school, she sat across from me at our gray and white Formica table while I ate the crispy sugar cookies she baked for my after school snack.

"Always make straight A's," she advised, "so no one can tell you you're not qualified to do something because you're a woman."

THE FIRST TIME I WENT GROCERY shopping with her in Houston, I went to the drinking fountain by myself and saw two separate fountains with big signs above them. One said "Colored." The other said "White." I felt ashamed drinking at the White fountain. When I found my mother in the aisles, I told her about the signs.

"Yes. I know," she said. "Mean white people put them there. They treat Negroes like they're not human. They make them sit at the back of the buses, too. When I came to this country and saw the Negroes sitting in the back of the buses, I wanted to leave. That's the way Hitler treated the Jews. But I couldn't go anywhere."

THUS, I WAS SEPARATED from my peers at an early age. Aware of my differences and that they mattered.

Of course, having a Dutch family already made me different from other kids—the language Tante Sonja, Uncle Rob, Moms, and my mother spoke to me, the pickled herring, cheese, and dark bread we ate. The way my Dutch mother dressed me probably pegged me as different to my peers, two long dangling braids with bows above them, brown and white saddle oxfords when everyone else wore penny loafers—and my name, Ingrid.

"I didn't want you to have a common name. I wanted you to be different," my mother told me.

I didn't mind being different. It made me feel special.

And despite being different, I played with kids at school, and made up a game on the playground, a game of tag in which a designated "giant" chased the rest of us who couldn't be tagged if we stood on an island—any patch of grass on the dirt playground. I also had a good friend at school who lived in a log cabin right down the street from our apartment. We went to each other's homes.

8

IF MY WORLD HAD BEEN DIVIDED, IT WOULD HAVE BEEN ENOUGH.

They also made it into a secret.

Again, my mother and I were alone in our apartment. My mother stood in the kitchen, a narrow room with short, yellow counters wedged between the refrigerator and stove and sink. I usually answered my mother's questions in that room while she cooked or washed dishes. What happened in school? Who were my friends? Was the test hard? What did I do at a friend's house? I never doubted how much she cared about me.

That morning, I carried the stack of breakfast plates to the sink where she was washing a frying pan. Daddy had already left for work. It was still school vacation.

"Ya. Put them right there, Ingridtje. That's great." She reached for a plate. I walked toward the kitchen door, toward my book. But she stopped me.

"Ingrid, there's something I want to tell you." I returned to stand beside her. Her hands—in rubber gloves—soaped and rinsed the square salmon colored plate.

"What?"

"You know . . . we're not going to tell anyone about The Shvantz." She put the plate in the drying rack and reached for another. "It's not something we want other people to know. We're just keeping it . . . inside our family." She reached a rubber gloved hand in the air to rub her nose with the side of her arm.

"People look down on you if you're divorced. We don't want people to know . . . about my divorce. Alright?"

"O.K."

You don't know when you agree to something how you might feel about it later. This seemed perfectly reasonable to me. I didn't really care. I couldn't see how it could affect me one way or the other. It was her divorce. It was her secret.

It did not become real to me until months later.

HELENE FROM MY CLASS AT SCHOOL lived in a house with a big back yard that sloped down a hill. This was the first time she'd asked me over. Her mother had called mine to invite me. I didn't talk to Helene much at school, so I had a lot to learn about her.

She'd suggested that we walk outside. I was following her, and I was feeling the strangeness of first times at friends' houses when you learn things you couldn't guess at school. We were almost at the bottom of that grassy hill in her back yard. The house looked small and distant. Helene led me in among a clump of gardenia bushes. Their dense scent surrounded us. She stopped and looked at me.

"My mommy's divorced," she said. She twisted the end of her ponytail around a finger.

"So's mine."

"C'mon. I'll race you up to the house. Mommy said there's a snack."

And there the conversation ended.

That afternoon I told my mother. She and I were setting the table for dinner before Daddy came home.

"Helene's mother's divorced." I thought the news would make her feel good. My mother wasn't the only one.

"How do you know?" Her tone was angry, suspicious.

"Helene told me. So I told her you were, too."

"You did!? But I told you not to tell anyone." She wailed the words at me.

"Yeah. But her mother's divorced, too. So what difference does it make if she knows?"

"Oh, Ingrid. You don't know what people are like. She might tell other people. And they'll look down on me. Adlai Stevenson didn't win the election for president, because he was divorced. I don't want you telling anyone. O.K.?"

"O.K., Mommy."

The whole thing seemed very serious. The opinions of others could be vicious and fierce. I could bring down something terrible on my mother by telling just one person about my father.

And so my father became a secret.

I WAS ALMOST SEVEN. I hadn't seen Lenny for two years. It didn't matter. We still talked and walked around together as if we hadn't been apart. Except for one moment—probably on the first day my parents and I arrived at his house. Lenny and I were in his bedroom looking at some kind of toy when he said, "Do you see Bay Tay?"

"Who's that?"

"Your father. That's what my parents and Moms call him, Bay Tay."

I realized what this meant—and I absorbed it.

Bay Tay. The Dutch pronunciation of my father's initials, B.T., for Bill Tyler. Tante Sonja, Uncle Rob, and Moms didn't refer to my father by his whole name, as if it were unspeakable. *Bay Tay* was code for "Ingrid's father."

I couldn't answer. I wasn't supposed to talk about my father to anyone. Did that mean Lenny? Did that mean other people in the family? I couldn't have talked to Lenny about my father even if I'd thought it was permitted in my mother's rule book. The existence of The Shvantz didn't belong here in this world with Lenny, his baby brother, David, Tante Sonja, Uncle Rob, and Moms. This was my safe world. This was the world where I lived with my parents. I couldn't mix the two worlds, not even with Lenny.

I saw the kind of look pass over Lenny's face that you see when someone realizes they shouldn't have said something. Lenny never mentioned my father again.

9

"WE'RE GOING ON A TRIP TO VISIT DADDY'S PARENTS. THEY'RE your Grandma and Grandpa. I want you to be a good girl."

"I will, Mommy."

It was the summer of my seventh birthday, our first full summer in Houston. On the drive, Daddy sang his usual songs. In the back seat, I read and took naps.

"WE'RE HERE, FOLKS!" Daddy parked in front of a brick house. My mother and I followed him up the steps of a small porch.

The second Daddy rang the bell, Grandma opened the door as if she'd been waiting on the other side. White curls framed her smiling face. She wore a light colored cotton dress belted at a somewhat broad waist below a big bosom. She hugged me the same way Aunt Julia did, with an enormous smile and her arms tight around me. "I am thrilled to finally meet this here granddaughter of mine!" My introduction to Grandma's soft, high pitched voice, her Yiddish accent, and her own brand of English.

I was happy to meet Grandma, too.

As she released me from her hug, I saw Grandpa, a short man with a rim of white hair around the edge of a bald head and a grin that made me feel he was about to share a joke just between us. Grandpa looked me in the eyes. "You made it alright then, on the long drive from Texas to Ontario?"

"Yes," I answered without hesitation. "I had a great book to read, and Daddy sang."

"O-o-oh!" Grandpa chuckled. "I can imagine what that was like!"

We laughed.

Grandma, Grandpa, and I fit together as if we always had been.

Every afternoon on the days Grandpa worked, Daddy would look at his watch, raise his eyebrows and state, "Oh! Say, Ingrid, Grandpa's walking down the sidewalk right now. It's time for you to meet him."

I'd scamper out the front door, down the porch steps, and see Grandpa a few blocks away in his navy blue uniform and hat. He'd raise his arm to wave, a big smile on his face. I'd run toward him on the sidewalk.

"It's the greatest thing to have my granddaughter come meet me," he'd say as we walked back side by side.

Grandpa was a subway conductor. Daddy said Grandpa was a brilliant man, but he never cared about earning money. Daddy said Grandpa was satisfied as long as he could read history at night—

and play checkers. One year, Grandpa was the checkers champion of Toronto.

On *Shabbat*, Grandma produced "the works" as Daddy called her dinner. The meal included an assortment of noodle dishes I saw for the first time at Grandma's table. My favorite was *kreplach*, a fried noodle dumpling filled with onions and potatoes.

THE SUMMER OF MY SIXTEENTH BIRTHDAY, I asked Grandma to teach me how to make *kreplach*. That day, right after I finished breakfast, Grandma called me into the kitchen. The room was warm with the smell of the chicken soup already simmering on the stove. Grandma tossed a heaping cup of flour, a few eggs, and several sprinkles of water into a brown ceramic mixing bowl. She dug her hands in and began to mix.

"Watch real careful. I don't have no recipe. I just know. Not too tough so's you have to work hard rolleeng it. Not too wet so's it sticks to your rolleeng pin. You mix it. You can't overdo mixing it."

While I kneaded the soft white dough in the bowl, Grandma sprinkled flour over a big wooden board and wiped her hands on a rolling pin.

She took the bowl from me, carried it over to the dusted board, plopped the dough into the middle of the board, and rolled vigorously.

"You have to roll it out thin. But don't get no holes in it.

"This here is how it should be. You feel it.

"While you ate breakfast, I fried some onions—two medium ones, chopped—in *schmaltz* and added mashed potatoes to the browned onions. See? If you don't have no chicken fat, you can use vegetable oil. But it don't taste as good. Now, watch how I fill the dough. Then, you finish."

Cutting the dough into squares, Grandma filled each one with a heaping spoonful of fried onions and potatoes and pinched the dough into a triangular dumpling.

"You make the rest. Then we'll fry them. With you doing that, I can start my strudel. Your father loves it." Grandma grinned at me.

MOST SUMMERS WE TOOK car trips to visit Grandma and Grandpa, with stops at all the relatives' homes. Often, my parents returned to Texas, and I remained at one of my aunt's and uncle's houses for a week.

In St. Louis, Uncle Joe made poached eggs on toast on Sundays. "This plate is for Ingy," he'd say when he handed me my plate. Only Uncle Joe used that nickname.

Tante Sonja took me and Lenny on adventures in D.C. At the Mint, we watched machines print thousands of green dollar bills onto huge slabs of paper. We took an elevator to the top of the Washington Monument and walked down. Lenny and I called out words to hear our voices echo.

During college, I spent Thanksgivings at Tante Nannie and Uncle Hal's house or Tante Sonja, Uncle Rob, and Moms' house instead of flying to Dallas from Massachusetts. Their homes became mine.

10

THE SHVANTZ CAME FOR ONE WEEK DURING MY SCHOOL Christmas vacation and one week in August, near my birthday. He picked me up every afternoon right after lunch and took me home right after dinner. Most of his visits were so similar they blur together, but I remember significant parts.

THE GRAY METAL SLATS of the venetian blinds gleamed white with dust in the sunlight of the picture window. The tote bag for my swim suit and book leaned against my chair by the window. I wanted to spend the afternoon curled in that chair, lost in a book, the way I'd spent many afternoons that summer, but The Shvantz was coming.

It was the August when I would be ten.

In the mornings that summer, except the few weeks spent visiting relatives, my mother and I had adventures. She took me to a clay workshop with a kiln where I sat at a long wooden table, molded bits of clay into doll cups, saucers, and plates, and applied glaze. Beside me, my mother painted mugs and plates with flowers and patterns. We left our creations to be fired.

Early in the summer, we had visited a knit shop. As my mother drove us there, she talked excitedly about her project. "I'm going to make a sequined sweater. They're the rage now, but very expensive.

"You'll see, Inky," she said, using the nickname Tante Nannie had given me. "I'll look gorgeous. You'll be proud of your mother.

"Moms used to take me, Tante Sonja, and Tante Nannie to the Bonneterie, the fanciest store in The Hague, to look at the latest styles. Then Moms hired a seamstress and told her what to make for each of us.

"I can't afford a seamstress. But I look in *Vogue* at the drugstore, and I look in the better dresses departments of Foleys and Sakowitz every season. That way I know the latest styles."

My mother made the clothes she longed for. I had watched her pin pattern pieces to swaths of material she'd laid on the dining room table. I loved the *swosh* of the scissors as she cut around the patterns.

"It's very important to look fashionable," she continued as we pulled into a parking space. "And to know how to dress. Never wear pink with red, or blue with green. In this country, people don't wear black after Memorial Day. And after Labor Day, they put their white clothes away."

I followed her into the dark store. Yarn-stuffed cubicles lined the walls from ceiling to floor. At the counter in front, my mother and a woman with a gray bun conferred while I wandered back to stare at the fleecy balls of magenta, turquoise, and mauve.

My mother chose white silk yarn and white, pearly sequins. She spent hours in the evenings knitting that sweater and sewing on the sequins. She sewed a flared black velvet skirt to go with it and wore the outfit all winter for fancy occasions.

My summer leisure had ended abruptly the day before when my mother called me over to the kitchen sink and said, "Tomorrow The Shvantz is coming."

Now, from my reading chair, I stared out the window on the first day of his one week visit. His rented car pulled up to the curb. I waited until he stood on the grass beside the car. Tall, much taller than the car, back straight, blonde-brown hair, blue eyes, he waited for me. Seeing Laurence Olivier always made me uneasy, because he looked so much like my father. But Olivier's demeanor seemed spritely. My father's was more wooden.

"Bye Mommy." Adding "He's here" seemed like too much of an acknowledgment of his existence.

My mother walked out of the kitchen and kissed me. "Goodbye schatje." She used a Dutch endearment that sounded like throat clearing.

"Hello, Honeybunch." My father leaned down to deliver a quick kiss on my cheek.

When he first started coming—that Christmas vacation when I was six—he walked around the car with me to help me in.

"Can I please get into the car by myself?" I had asked one day after I told my parents about my discomfort at his assistance, at his hovering too near. They'd advised me to ask that question.

"Of course, Honeybunch," he'd answered.

I'd felt awkward and uncomfortable asking a question I considered to be cruel. Cruel, because he wanted to be near me. I hated telling him he couldn't. But since then, he'd let me get into the car myself like I did in my parents' cars.

Today as I settled on the front seat beside him, he asked his usual question.

"How was your summer, Honeybunch?"

"Fine," I mumbled softly, in my much as you're going to get out of me voice.

On the drive to the motel, he said, "I wrote a new song (s-a-a-w-n-g) I'd like to sing to you." He pulled himself up behind the steering wheel, took a deep breath, puffed up his chest, and began.

My father spoke with exaggerated pronunciation. The exaggeration was worse when he sang, which he often did. On words like sound and round he opened his mouth as if he were swallowing a baseball. S-o-w-w-n-d, he sang. R-o-w-w-n-d. Deep, slow, precise pronunciation. Over controlled. Not a deep rich baritone that makes you feel like flying when you listen, but over modulated tones that remind of being too clean, too good, too polite—tones that constrict flight. That remind of a young man cowed by his mother, sitting at an elderly aunt's tea table, his back straight, his sips of tea careful, his cake cut into slivers with the side of his fork and chewed many times.

It was the exaggerated expression of a person ill at ease in the social situation. Not surprising, since I didn't make conversation easy for him. He knew nothing of my school, friends, or interests. I wouldn't tell him I spent hours with a box of pastels rubbing the chartreuse, magenta, and royal blue of my fantasies onto blank pieces of paper, or that I danced to a record of *Swan Lake* and choreographed it in my imagination, or that I roamed for hours through the tall weeds in the field behind our apartment complex, ate what the kids on the farm down the road called "dew berries" off thorny vines, and stooped over the luminous petals of a bright red cactus flower to see the deep, sticky insides.

The Houston heat lay heavy most of the year. Winters might reach as low as the seventies, maybe sixties some days, but summer climbed up around a hundred and stayed there. Palm trees and magnolias grew in that heat. Gardenias and honey suckle perfumed the air. In the middle of the city, moss covered trees leaned over bayous—narrow water-filled ravines that wound through an elite cluster of grand old houses and passed the Medical Center and nearby zoo, the area where we lived. A large mechanical "grasshopper" moved up and down drilling for oil not far from the majestic hulks of the Prudential Building and the Shamrock Hotel. We passed these structures to reach my father's motel.

The sun shimmered off the cement around the kidney shaped pool at the motel. I stepped on the back of my saddle oxfords to remove them and pulled off my socks. The cement burned my feet as I walked toward the pool, head down, careful not to look at my father. Book in hand, I eased myself into the tepid water. I stood on the side of the pool farthest from my father's chair and read, my barrier against him, my way to make time pass quickly. As usual, he hadn't even changed into a swim suit. While I read, he sat beside the pool and talked to the other grownups, if there were any.

That's how he'd met Kathy's parents one summer. They were moving to Houston, staying in the motel while they looked for a place to live. My father kept in touch with them, and we went to their house one afternoon during each of his visits.

Kathy was just about my age, with chin length curly brown hair, warm brown eyes, and an impish appearance as if she were about to laugh.

Kathy and her parents lived in a house in a part of Houston far from the apartments where my parents and I lived. Trees surrounded Kathy's house. In the backyard, there was a play house, a wooden extravaganza of ladders and rooms, with a slide attached. The existence of this playhouse in anyone's backyard seemed like a fantasy to me who saved a penny a week to buy a *Little Lulu* to read on my rollaway bed.

The first summer I went to Kathy's house with my father, I tried to hide silently in Kathy's stash of Donald Duck comic books. But Kathy wanted me to play with her and her little sister in the playhouse.

"Come on. Can't catch me!" she goaded. Kathy ran, and I let her. She returned to her bedroom where I sat on the carpet by her bookcase.

"Come on! Let's go outside to the playhouse! You'll like it. You'll see."

I gave up and followed her down the hall and through the back door.

"Let's chase each other up the ladder and down the slide," Kathy shouted. I went through the motions, slowly, like a sleepwalker, trying not to be mean to her, but saying as little as possibly required to play whatever she wanted.

At all times with my father, I was in a world that did not exist in my other world. I, however, was real, even in this secret world that seemed to float outside of time and space, like a fantasy. But my ability to react changed. I watched—as if I were inside a bubble—so that nothing in this world could affect me. But I was not so altered that I could be consciously cruel.

I did not know—or did not admit—that not talking to my father, not recognizing his presence, not sharing any feelings with him, was one of the cruelest things I could do. Even if I had admitted this, it wouldn't have mattered. Anything I did in this dimension had no repercussions in the one I lived in. Besides, my parents knew I wasn't talking to my father, and they liked it.

HE TOOK ME TO DINNER before he took me home.

He always took me to the same place, a cut above a fast food restaurant. We slid into a booth beside a jukebox. My father faced my silence.

"What would you like, Honeybunch?"

I always had fried chicken or a hamburger, and fries. *Let him ask me.*

"How about fried chicken, French fries, and a milk shake?"

"O.K."

"Would you like to pick a song?" I couldn't believe it when he asked me this each time. He meant the jukebox.

My parents wouldn't waste money in a jukebox. A nickel pushed down a slot. And for what? For rock 'n roll.

"O.K." I agreed. My father inserted a nickel.

"Pick a title you want to hear and press the button."

The choice was easy. I reached up and pushed the button for "Blue Suede Shoes."

I loved Elvis' music and even received a record of his from Moms, despite my mother's railing against rock 'n roll as "junk," and Daddy's deriding Elvis' swaying hips and his fans' screaming and fainting as "a lot of *meshugas*" (the Yiddish word for craziness).

"He's trying to drive them all crazy with that pelvis of his, and he's succeeding," Daddy laughed derisively when Elvis crooned on Ed Sullivan. "Yes, sir. Elvis the pelvis really knows how to manipulate those dumb girls. Look at them, will ya? Fools!"

I would not have screamed or ripped off my blouse, but that crooning sent me, as young as age nine, though much more modestly. I simply sat in our living room, turned on my record, and sang along, feeling slightly guilty for liking something that trivial and lowly.

Sitting in the booth beside the jukebox, I pulled off a crusty piece of fried chicken and listened to Elvis. The food and Elvis barely made sitting across from my father tolerable. The only thing in my mind: *If I can get through this, I'll be home soon.*

MY PARENTS WERE EATING when I entered. "Do you want anything, Inky?" My mother, Tante Sonje, Tante Nannie, Moms, and Grandma all pushed food. In their homes, meals were an occasion, a time for everyone to gather, not just to assuage hunger of the body, but of the soul. The adults sat around the dinner table for hours, debating politics, weighing issues that affected Israel, and telling jokes.

"I'm full."

"What did he give you to eat? Where did he take you?" Her features tightened a bit as I answered. I didn't mention the jukebox.

"What did he eat?"

I thought back to that booth, the jukebox blaring, my dipping French fries into ketchup. "Nothing, I guess."

"Don't you know?"

"I don't remember him eating anything."

"I see," my mother said in her arch tone. "Tomorrow, ask him where he eats, and ask him to take you there."

THE CURTIS STEAK HOUSE, a low-ceilinged, sprawling place. The hostess seated my father across from me at a white covered table with stemmed water glasses and fresh flowers. Only one other couple was eating that early.

"I usually have shrimp cocktail. Would you like to try it?"

I loved shrimp but had only eaten them once. Shrimp were expensive and my mother, the source of our only fancy meals, didn't want to stand in the kitchen for hours deveining the slimy creatures. So there in the Curtis Steak House, I said I would like to have shrimp cocktail.

I liked the sharp cocktail sauce almost more than the plump chewy shrimp. We ate silently, each looking down at our food. When we finished, my father suggested fruit cocktail "for dessert."

"Shrimp cocktail and fruit cocktail are my favorite foods," he informed me.

The small cut glass bowl contained canned squares of peaches and pears, grapes that fell off my spoon, and a piece of maraschino cherry. My first fruit cocktail.

"THAT'S ALL HE GAVE YOU! I bet he usually eats more than that."

My mother's derision had to be aimed at me. I had done her bidding, only to disappoint her. Whenever I disappointed her, I was sure it was the Shvantzness in me. If my father was a Shvantz, some part of me had to be a Shvantz, too.

MY MOTHER HAD ANOTHER IDEA for The Shvantz after my dinner at the steak house.

My favorite toys were dolls, and the ones I coveted—stared at in the toy stores for as long as my parents would allow—were the Madam Alexanders. Their faces shone. Their hair looked real. Their costumes were detailed. I especially wanted the ones based on the characters from *Little Women*. Madam Alexander dolls, according to my parents, cost "a small mint."

"Why don't you ask The Shvantz for a Madam Alexander doll?" my mother suggested the evening after the Curtis Steak House escapade. "I'm sure he wants to buy you a present."

ONCE, I DARED TO TELL MY MOTHER I wanted a bra for my doll, but I didn't outright ask. Probably they were being advertised on television during the Saturday morning cartoon shows. My mother bought me one. I ran into my room to put it on my doll, but the bra was for a much bigger doll. It flopped around on my doll's chest. My excitement at receiving this bra turned to disappointment. I didn't tell my mother.

A few days later, my mother came into my bedroom while I was playing and asked how I liked the bra.

"It doesn't fit," I said.

"Ya!? That's how you talk to your mother? In that tone of voice? I've told you never to talk back to me."

She left my room for a moment and returned with a brown leather belt. She wrapped the buckle part around her fist, left the leather dangling, pulled down my pants and delivered leather slaps to my bare behind.

"That's how you talk to your mother who went through all that trouble to buy you something you wanted? All that expense. Not even a thank you? No. You throw in my face your complete lack of appreciation."

"What did I do?!" I sobbed. "All I did was tell you the truth. The bra doesn't fit."

She left the room. I lay down on my bed and sobbed into my pillow. I was stunned. She'd never hit me with a belt. And why now? All I'd done was tell her the truth when I answered her question. I sobbed at the injustice and decided I would never forget what my mother had just done. I would never be unfair to my own child.

BUT IT WAS THIS SAME MOTHER who told me to ask The Shvantz for a doll that cost "a small mint."

I found the words, terse, simple, without emotion.

"Daddy?" What elation he must have felt at the appellation. I usually avoided addressing him, and certainly, with that title.

"I was wondering. Would you buy me a present?"

Maybe he wanted to reward me for finally acknowledging his paternity, or maybe just for saying anything at all. "We-e-e-ll,

Sweetheart, let's see-e-e. What exactly were you thinking of? I'd have to see if it fits into what I was counting on spending for this trip."

"I'd really like a Madam Alexander doll."

"We-e-ll, I don't know what they are. But I suppose there'd be no harm in looking at one, just to get an idea."

"They have them at Foley's in the toy department."

In Foley's, I stood beside him on the escalator and looked up at him when I talked. I usually avoided eye contact. I felt strange, uncomfortable, divorced from this performance in which I told him how to get to the toy department and where the dolls were.

"I'd like to see the Jo doll," I told the sales lady. She unlocked the glass case and took the doll down from her pedestal. Jo was in my hands. I burned with excitement. I raised plaintive eyes toward my father and said nothing.

"How much is the doll?" he enunciated slowly to the sales lady.

I held my breath as the sales lady answered.

"We-e-ll, is this something you really have your heart set on, Honeybunch?"

"Yes." Softly spoken. I looked into his eyes again.

"O.K. Well, just this time, then. Please wrap it up for her."

Jo was mine! I'd won so easily.

I left the Foley's toy department with the box in my hands, walking beside my father without speaking, my victory tinged with a mixture of disdain for his being so easily manipulated and of guilt at finagling this success. I knew it was bad to ask for presents. But I asked. And he bought it. I conned my father. I could do this in my secret world, the world that didn't exist.

"Did he buy you the doll?" My mother's eyes were full of expectation. I'd barely entered the apartment. I held up the box.

"Wonderful, Inky!"

I lifted the lid.

"Oh, the doll is gorgeous," she said.

11

IN FIRST GRADE I STARTED RELIGIOUS SCHOOL AT TEMPLE Emanuel, the congregation in Houston for Reform Jews. The first Sunday my mother drove me there, she gave me her explanation of Reform Judaism, "Reform Jews decide which Jewish rules they'll follow."

She explained that joining Temple Emanuel was my parents' grand compromise. In The Hague, she'd been raised Orthodox. Her family kept kosher and didn't work on *Shabbat*. Now she didn't want to follow those rules anymore. But she did want to go to services, especially on the holidays. Daddy's family never kept kosher or went to services. He had agreed to go with her to the shorter Reform services.

I looked out the car window as we passed the hulk of the Shamrock Hotel and the surrounding palm trees.

OURS WAS A JUDAISM woven out of ethics and embroidered with my mother's memories of her family's observance of *Shabbat* and the Jewish holidays and with Daddy's memories of Grandma's cooking. Daddy added the history that drove Grandma and Grandpa out of Eastern Europe to Canada from places with fantastic names, Grodno Gubernia, where Grandpa came from, and Galicia, where Grandma came from. At young ages they arrived in Toronto. My grandfather, around age eight with his siblings and mother. My grandmother, around age ten, alone, to be met by her older sister and introduced to a sewing machine in a sweatshop and to an attic room where the two sisters lived in the house of an Italian family.

His parents were driven out by pogroms, Daddy explained, as he gave me his description of pogroms: Cossacks on horseback and neighboring villagers entered Jewish towns, eager to stab, burn, and kill Jews.

Grandma and Grandpa met in Toronto through Labor Zionist organizations, Daddy said. Grandpa was in the Farbund. He delivered lectures in Yiddish about world history—not just about Jews—and current politics. Grandma was in the Pioneer Women.

Often at the dinner table, Daddy would say we had to learn from the bad things done to the Jews and not allow other people to be treated that way. When I was a teenager, Daddy leaned toward me across the dinner table one night and said, "Listen, Ingrid, if we ever believe people in this country want to wipe out all the Black people like Hitler tried to wipe out all the Jews, we'll hide as many Black people as we can in our house, see? That's what we'd have to do."

Israel was an important topic of conversation in our home. The Jews need our own country, he said, because of the pogroms and the Holocaust—and antisemitism in so many places. Daddy made sure I knew Israeli history. Especially that all the surrounding Arab countries attacked Israel when Israel declared it was a state in 1948. What the Israelis need most, he emphasized, is recognition of Israel's right to exist. Israel's early leaders, like Ben Gurion and Golda Meir, were household names. One of Daddy's favorite stories was that he sat on Golda's lap in the back of a car when he was a very young boy, when she still lived in Wisconsin, way before she was Prime Minister of Israel.

"If there had been an Israel during The War," my mother said one day, "Jews would have had a country to go to."

Once I accused Daddy of never teaching me anything about Judaism. He didn't hesitate. "Why that's not so. Not so at all.

"Ingrid, when I talk to you at dinner about the right way to treat people, I'm teaching you to be a good Jew."

THE FIRST DAY OF RELIGIOUS school I met Marcie. She sat at the desk beside the one I was about to take. We looked at each other. Two blond haired, blue eyed girls with braids (hers without bows above them) and saddle oxfords. It was as if all the similarities in our families were written on our faces for us to see in that instant. Democratic politics. Abhorrence of Joe McCarthy. Abhorrence of racism. Her aunt and my mother, both Holocaust survivors. Our grandmothers' childhood emigrations out of Poland to North America. Marcie's parents taught religious school on Sundays. My mother taught Hebrew school on weekday afternoons. We sat beside each other that day and for the rest of our years together at Temple Emanuel.

"There's a girl in my class I want to ask over," I told my mother when she picked me up that first morning.

WHEN WE ENTERED MY ROOM, Marcie plopped on the floor by my bookcase and combed through my comic books. I walked over to my dolls.

"You can play dolls if you want," she said. "I don't care. I want to read comic books."

I didn't mind. It was comfortable doing what we each wanted to do when we were together. Sometimes we just sat and read our books.

MY PARENTS TOOK ME to see the movie of *Guys and Dolls*, and they bought the record. Marcie and I danced to the songs in our apartment.

"We have to kick our legs in the air at the same time, just like they did in the movie." I showed her, and we pretended to be in a chorus line. We danced to Frank Sinatra records at her house.

THE FIRST TIME WE SPENT the night together, she said, "I have to say my prayers now. I say them every night before I go to sleep."

"Do you say them out loud?"

"No. In my mind. I ask God to bless everyone in my family. I name them. And I ask God to bless me."

"Me, too," I said. "I talk to God in my mind before I go to sleep. I ask him to bless my parents and me. I've never told anyone about this before. I never knew anyone I wanted to tell something so personal."

"Me either," she said. "O.K. Let's say our prayers now."

MARCIE BECAME MY BEST FRIEND. "We're sisters," we told each other.

Our parents found each other through us. They sat around each other's dinner tables for hours, discussing politics and playing bridge. Marcie's father, a thin, tall man, well over six feet, would fold himself into a chair around the dining room table, look over at Daddy with excitement shining from his eyes behind heavy framed glasses, and he would say, "You know, Benny, I've got something to tell you." With that he'd launch into whatever topic was on his mind, usually something in the news or an ethical issue. Marcie and I knew we got our real education around those dinner tables.

MARCIE, HER PARENTS, and older brother, Frank, took me crabbing with them in Galveston one summer. They showed me how to wrap hamburger meat in a piece of her mother's old stockings, tie this into a little bag at the end of a string, and dangle the bag over the side of the pier until I felt a tug on the string.

"Let me know now when you feel a tug, and I'll catch the little fella with this net." Marcie's father held up a long stick with a net on one end.

At the first tug, I yelled, "I have one!" I held my breath and leaned way over the pier to pull up the wiggling little crab. Its claws were stuck in my stocking bag. By late afternoon, we filled the cooler in the trunk of the car with crabs and ice and headed back to Houston.

On the drive home, Frank sat on the back seat of the car between me and Marcie and peeled his sunburnt skin all over the floor.

"Frank! I'm sorry. That's making me sick," Marcie said. "You stop that right now!"

We passed around a big bag of chocolate chip cookies and finished it by the time we reached Marcie's house.

MY FAMILY MOVED TO DALLAS when Marcie and I were in junior high school. Marcie's parents often drove up with Marcie and Frank to stay with us. Sometimes Marcie and her cousin took the Greyhound bus up from Houston to stay with us for a week, or I went down to stay with her family in Houston.

Our families were always in touch. But never did I mention to Marcie what I did during the week of our Christmas vacations or one week each August.

12

MOMS OFTEN TOLD ME AND MY COUSINS, "FAMILY IS THE MOST important thing you have." She wanted us to be close.

Tante Sonja, Tante Nannie, and my mother wanted that, too. They decided the cousins would be together every summer. Lenny and I—and later Lenny's little brother, David—never went to camp like other kids. We went for two weeks every summer to stay with Tante Nannie, Uncle Hal, and their kids, our younger cousins, Nancy and Rachel—and later, their younger sister, Yvette—at their house in Connecticut. Those two weeks were the closest I came to having brothers and sisters for the first fourteen years of my life, before my brother was born.

Tante Nannie and Uncle Hal's house was built on the steep slope of a hill. A woods stretched up behind the screen porch in the back. Thick trunked stately cedar trees stood among tall swaying pine, sassafras, maple and oak. I learned to recognize the leaves of those trees in a class at the nearby Nature Center. The woods behind the house felt familiar. I knew I belonged there.

Right at the edge of the woods, beside the screen porch door, two ragged edged rocks, nearly four feet in height and almost parallel to each other, jutted toward the tree tops. Gray streaked the basic black of those rocks and mica flecked their surfaces. Velvet green moss grew in their niches and around their bases. These were not the only rocks in that woods. A barely perceptible path of pine needles and Connecticut dirt wound up the hill behind the two rocks to another larger, humpy rock deep under the trees, a perfect reading seat far away from the noises inside the house.

Those two nearly parallel rocks outside the screen porch became the focal point of many summers when we three cousins visited Tante Nannie and Uncle Hal. Lenny and I discovered them the first summer. "Look at these two rocks!" I said. "I bet we can fit in between them. Let's clear out the space and build a fort."

I stuck my hand right into the pile of leaves and sticks and started pulling them out.

"After that stuff is gone," Lenny said, "we can cover the floor with pine needles to make it soft."

We both worked steadily. Lenny scooped pine needles off the floor of the woods and carried them down to the fort. Once the leaves and sticks were gone, I scraped down the floor with a stick.

"It looks good enough now, Ingrid." Lenny showed me how we should spread the pine needles on the floor of the fort to make it neat and soft enough to sit on. I helped him.

"We're done!" he pronounced.

We sat inside.

"It's really comfortable," Lenny said.

"Yeh," I leaned sideways against one of the rocks.

"But we need a roof," Lenny decided.

"OK. What should we use?"

Lenny suggested long sticks. I said we should cover them with wet leaves from under trees in the woods. That would keep the sticks together and keep out rain.

The roof was the hardest part. We had to get sticks that were long enough to fit across and figure out how to balance them. It took us all the next day to get the roof right.

It was harder to fit inside with the roof on. We had to scrunch down a little.

I said we should pretend bad guys were running through the woods, and we could hide from them in our fort. And sometimes we could eat our peanut butter and jelly sandwiches in there.

We played in our fort every day, even if we went to the beach or the Nature Center that day.

The next summer we had trouble fitting into the fort and had to figure out a way to make the roof higher.

Everything we did together in Connecticut felt exciting to me. We went to a beach in a cove and swam out to a floating pier. Tante Nannie brought peanut butter and jelly sandwiches and apples for a picnic. The bookmobile visited the neighborhood. Lenny and I chased the big white truck down the street until it stopped. We climbed inside to explore the shelves of books along the narrow aisle. Lenny checked out Hardy Boys books and I got Nancy Drew. I usually took my books up the hill to the reading rock, but on rainy days we sat inside and read and wrote book reports for Tante Nannie.

THOUGH MOMS LIVED with Tante Sonja, Uncle Rob, Lenny, and Daniel in Virginia, she visited her other daughter's homes for a few months every year. In the summers, she took a ship to the Netherlands. She returned with a suitcase full of *zoute drop*, Dutch salty licorice. We craved *zoute drop* and couldn't find it in candy stores in this country.

WE COUSINS PILED OUT of the back of the station wagon to follow Uncle Hal and Tante Nannie from the parking lot over to the dock. We'd come to meet Moms when her ship returned to New York City. Moms walked down the gangplank to the dock like a queen. Dressed in a dark gray suit and black medium high heels, she approached us slowly, her head held high, her face radiating a smile that seemed meant for each of us. At the end of the gangplank, she held out her arms and laughed with happiness as she hugged us individually.

We followed Uncle Hal to claim Moms' luggage out of the piles of suitcases. It was a family joke that Moms' luggage, alone, made one huge pile. We kids couldn't wait to see what was inside, and we felt so comfortable with Moms we didn't hesitate to ask the important question.

Right there on the dock, while Uncle Hal loaded Moms' suitcases onto a dolly, I asked, "Moms, did you bring *zoute drop*?" With Moms I could do things I could never do with my mother.

"What do you think? Of course I have *drop* for everyone!" Another big smile.

On the way back to Connecticut in the car, Moms said in a few days she would take us to Radio City Music Hall. "We'll see a good movie, and we'll visit a bakery," she promised.

WE MUST HAVE GONE to Tante Nannie and Uncle Hal's until a year or two before Lenny started college. He was the first of us to go. After our summers at Tante Nannie and Uncle Hal's, the cousins saw each other at least once a year.

As important as we were in each other's lives, my cousins never asked about my father. And I never mentioned him to them, to Moms, or to my aunts and uncles.

13

I WATCHED MY MOTHER MELT THE BOTTOM OF THE FIRST CANDLE to secure it in the menorah. This would be my first *Chanukah*. I was six years old.

"Many American Jews make a big deal out of *Chanukah*," she said. "They don't want their children to feel cheated because they're not getting a big Christmas tree with decorations and lots of presents."

Chanukah, she explained, is not really a very important Jewish holiday. Some families give one present every night, but presents have nothing to do with *Chanukah*. She and Daddy would give me one small present, because it's fun.

"We Jews don't have to compete with Christmas," my mother stated proudly. "We're lucky. We have way more holidays to celebrate than the Christians do."

I thought of Aunt Julia's taking me to my first *Purim* festival. My mother was right about our wonderful holidays.

Only a few weeks after this *Chanukah* conversation, I discovered a very personal link with my Jewishness when my first baby tooth fell out and I followed my mother's instructions to stick it under my pillow. She said a tooth fairy might take my tooth during the night and leave me something special.

As soon as I woke up, I reached under my pillow and found a piece of paper wrapped around something hard. It was a dime wrapped in a note that read:

Dear Ingrid, Thank you for your tooth. Love, The *Yiddische* Fairy

"Was there anything under your pillow this morning?" my mother asked at breakfast.

I laughed and looked at her. "The *Yiddische* Fairy left me a dime for my tooth!"

"How did you know who left it?"

"Because she wrote me a note."

Daddy chimed into the game, "Oh yeah? The *Yiddische* Fairy, aye? She's the best tooth fairy there is."

"Especially since she's Mommy!" I laughed.

"How do you know that?" my mother asked.

"She has your handwriting!"

We all burst into loud, satisfying laughter.

THE *YIDDISCHE* FAIRY HAD LEFT me many notes and dimes before my father's most memorable Christmas visit. I must have been ten or eleven when it occurred.

At the beginning of that Christmas vacation, my mother suggested our annual trip downtown to look at the Christmas decorations in the department stores. Elaborate displays of elves' workshops and Christmas trees surrounded by toys—even working electric trains—filled the store windows and lobbies.

"Look, Inky!" My mother pointed at a stuffed animal monkey on a swing.

"Mommy, look at the elf hammering!" I glanced at her to be sure she saw it.

Christmas music filled the air. "I love this music," my mother said.

I liked the music, too, and I was happy she was giving me permission to enjoy it, even if it wasn't for our holiday.

There on the sidewalk with the Christmas music filtering around us and a big Christmas tree in the store window beside us, my mother told me that when people talk about tolerance, what they mean is "I'll tolerate people if they are like me.

"Real tolerance," she said, "is accepting people's differences. Differences make the world interesting."

My father came to town the next day.

On the afternoon of the event that made this visit so memorable, we arrived in his motel room after seeing a Disney movie. The small room was filled with a narrow dresser, double bed, and two straight backed chairs beside a tiny round table. I sat on a chair.

He walked over to the dresser and picked up a black book. It was the book known to me as the Christian Bible. He did this every Christmas vacation. He read me the story of the birth of Jesus.

This year, I spoke. "Please, don't read that to me." I gave no explanation. I didn't say that I'm Jewish and when he reads to me from the Christian Bible, I feel awful because it's not part of my religion. Maybe if I'd explained, he would have told me I was baptized as a Methodist at birth, and that made me a Methodist. If only I could have talked to him, maybe I would have told him that I respected his religion and wished he would respect mine. Could he have accepted that his daughter was Jewish, when his religion was so important to him?

I ran into the bathroom. He followed me and stood in the bathroom doorway to block my escape. All six foot three of him loomed over me, stern, foreboding, like Cotton Mather.

"Sit down!" he commanded and pointed to the closed toilet.

I stood still. The situation was ludicrous. And I did not want anything to do with that book.

"Sit down!"

I remained standing. He advanced toward me. "Sit down. Or I'll turn you over my knee." A thing he'd never done and never threatened before.

He was a monstrous tremble of rage bent toward me. I sat on the hard surface of the closed toilet seat. He sat across from me on the bathtub edge, put the book on his gargantuan knees, and began to read, slowly enunciating every word in his deep baritone.

MARCIE AND I SAT on the rag rug in her bedroom, between us a wooden case that unfolded to become a Chinese checkers board. "My cousins and my aunt and uncle came down from Pennsylvania over Christmas vacation," Marcie said. "They brought me this.

"Frank and I played Chinese checkers with our cousins every day at the kitchen table. We also went ice skating and saw some movies."

Marcie looked up from the Chinese checkers board on the floor between us.

"What did you do over Christmas vacation?" she asked.

"Oh, nothing. I read some books."

14

DADDY LEFT RESEARCH AT M.D. ANDERSON AND OPENED HIS OWN office as a general surgeon. My mother worked in the office instead of teaching Hebrew school. We moved out of the apartment into a house, and I started seventh grade with a new group of kids from a different elementary school.

Right before my thirteenth birthday, I announced to my parents at dinner, "I'm almost a teenager. From now on, I'm calling you Mom and Dad."

"That makes good sense," my mother said. "You're really growing up."

Dad grinned. "Well, well, well. My big girlie, almost a teenager. You may certainly call me Dad."

That August, as usual, my father came to Houston.

On the first day, as soon as I sat in the car, he said, "Honeybunch, I want to tell you the news in my life.

"I met a woman in my choir named Dottie. After singing in the choir together for a long time, we decided to get married. Dottie came with me this time. She wants to meet you. She's waiting for us at the motel right now."

I didn't reply.

"I think you'll like her."

Silence. I didn't care what he did.

At my father's knock, Dottie opened the door. She was tall, a few inches shorter than my father, angular, a bit flat faced with high, broad cheek bones. She had earlobe length wavy brown hair, pressed against her head, and parted on one side, not a bouffant like the poofy bubbles my mother and her friends backcombed and sprayed their hair into. Dottie wore a short sleeved, scooped neck dress—white with a royal blue flower print—and at her throat, two rows of chunky white beads. Though not fat, she slouched in a manner that caused her abdomen to protrude and hang.

Newly thirteen and well-schooled by my mother on the latest styles, I privately sneered at Dottie's old fashioned look.

"We-e-e-ll, I'm so happy to meet you, Ingrid"

I shifted my eyes to the floor and replied softly, "Thank you."

"Honeybunch, Dottie and I have a song we'd like to sing for you," my father announced. "I composed it myself. Take a seat."

I found the only chair. My father and Dottie stood formally at the other end of the small room. My father blew on a pitch pipe. They both hummed the note and launched into the song, my father in his over enunciated manner, Dottie's high pitched voice warbling off the apparent melody. The words were about a manger in someone's heart.

I lowered my head and pulled into myself, far away from that song.

At the end, my father spoke. "I want to tell you a story about some children we've befriended in our neighborhood. Dottie and I go for walks in a park near our house, and we've met some children there. One of the boys is named Donald. There are also several little girls. One day, I asked the girls if they would like to see Donald Duck. They all said, 'Yes.' So, I turned to Donald, swung my arm toward him, and he ducked. The girl's got the joke."

Dottie let out a little chuckle, "Heh, heh."

I stared at him.

That afternoon we went to the zoo. Dottie wore white gloves and carried a small flat purse on a chain over her forearm.

I DESCRIBED DOTTIE to my parents that evening. I emphasized her hanging abdomen and restrained personality. It was fun to make them laugh.

Jealousy of The Shvantz's new wife was not an issue. I knew how strong my parents' marriage was. Dad often told the story about how he met my mother. He was doing a general surgery residency in D.C. One of the other residents, a Dutch woman, had a party. "I saw Mummy across the room and thought she was the most beautiful woman I'd ever seen."

But she was on her way out when he saw her. Dad didn't let that stop him.

"Tante Nannie was at that party, too, because she was a friend of the Dutch hostess," he explained. "I knew she was Mummy's sister, so I asked her for Mummy's phone number."

My mother always intervened here. "The hostess asked Dad to that party because she was after him. But he asked me out instead!"

They dated every weekend and married three months after they met.

My mother told me privately many times, "Dad's the smartest man I ever met, and he's my best friend. Don't get married until you find your best friend."

I loved their love.

15

October of eighth grade. My mother and I were putting away groceries. Tomato soup can in hand, she turned to me. "Inky, would you like to have another person in our family?"

I looked at her waistline, slim as ever. "Why? Are you pregnant or something?"

"Or something!" She laughed. "Yes. I'm pregnant!"

"Oh, I hope I have a baby brother!"

She laughed again. "We'll see what we get. I'm glad you're happy."

That wasn't the only change. Dad decided to give up his medical practice as a general surgeon. We were moving to Dallas where he'd do a residency to become a head and neck surgeon. I'd start the second semester of eighth grade there.

In late December, my mother, Moms, and I climbed into my mother's musty car which had a U-Haul attached to the back. I squeezed into the narrow space left between the boxes on the back seat and floor.

Beside my mother in the front seat, Moms wore her mink coat. That mink coat and a strand of pearls were the two things Moms had decided demonstrated upper middle class status in the United States. She had lost the upper middle class life she'd lived in The Hague—her house full of Persian carpets, porcelain dishes, silver platters and candlesticks, elegant ornaments, and paintings. Her wardrobe made by seamstresses in all the latest fashions. Her servant who shopped, cooked, and cleaned. Her prosperous shoe store in The Hague's business district. My grandfather's two movie theaters. Moms had recently acquired the coat. "Real mink!" she declared to each of us in the extended family the first time we saw her wear it. A few years later, she would acquire the pearl necklace.

Dad had already started the residency in Dallas. We would meet him at our new home.

About two hours into the drive, rain began pounding on the car and stayed with us. We reached the outskirts of Dallas by dark. The rain turned to ice.

"I can't get the ice off the windshield." My mother leaned as far forward as her belly allowed to see through the streaks of ice.

"The wipers are stuck! I can't see the road."

"Sienike," Moms said, using the Dutch ending *ke* to express affection for my mother. "We have to pull over."

"Yah. You're right. But we can't sit in this car. It's too cold."

"We'll hitchhike," Moms declared.

My mother pulled onto the shoulder. She and Moms opened their doors and stepped out. I climbed over the boxes and joined them. We stood on the icy shoulder of the highway. Two women—one three months pregnant, one in her seventies, pulling the collar of her mink coat up around her neck—and one thirteen year old girl, clutching her book. Freezing rain pelted our bare heads. Moms, a head shorter than I, straightened her shoulders, lifted her chin, and stuck her arm straight up in the air.

A car pulled over. The lone man inside leaned over to crank down the window on the passenger side. "Where y'all headed?"

"Dallas," my mother said and gave him the main streets.

"Get on in, y'all. I can take you there."

We abandoned the over packed car and the rented U-Haul on the side of the highway for this stranger's heated car.

It was late at night when we pulled up to the pink brick house that would become my home for the next three years. We thanked the stranger who had saved us and found our way over the icy sidewalk to the doorbell. Dad threw open the door. "Oh, is it good to see you!" he said. He and Mom drove back in the morning to rescue our still intact over-packed car and the U-Haul.

MY MOTHER AND I stood in the kitchen of that pink house. She snipped tips off of string beans. I set the kitchen table.

"You're not as close to any girls here in Dallas as you were to Marcie," my mother said. She plunged the green beans into boiling water. She would say that many times after we moved to Dallas.

A NOISE OUTSIDE THE WINDOW of my high school English class. A yell, a slam, a siren? I don't remember. I remember everyone else in the class ran to the window. I stayed at my desk.

"You never did what everyone else did. The day we all rushed to the window during English to see what the noise was, you sat at your desk. I wondered about that." One of the boys who'd been in my high school English class asked me this when we became friends during winter break freshman year of college.

Why did I stay at my desk?

Even though the braids were eventually cut off and the saddle oxfords abandoned. Even though I, too, had a bouffant hairdo and could do the twist, I was different from other kids.

The Holocaust made me different. No one around me had heard of it. We didn't learn in history classes about the Nazis' carefully planned, industrialized genocide of the Jewish people—that even we Jews can barely believe. It wasn't in common day parlance until 1978 when *Holocaust* was on TV. I knew of evil, had Hell in my background, knew about the worst of which people are capable. I had to be vigilant against that evil. This required a removal from group behavior—a duty I respected.

But there's rarely one reason for anything. There was also the overarching secret at the core of my existence. A major part of my life was not real. I was different.

MY MOTHER WAS RIGHT. I didn't feel as close to any girls in Dallas as I did to Marcie. I would never find any I felt as comfortable with. But there was more. I'd learned how to keep a significant issue in my life secret from my closest friend. I'd learned to be with someone and be alone.

The secrecy became addictive. It spread to other topics. I could sit with someone who was confiding in me and appear completely engaged but never convey anything beneath the surface of my own life. I talked about books, movies, politics, and school—and gave lots of advice, so I never had to get too close.

I did have girlfriends in Dallas, girls I invited over to spend the night. Girls with whom I shared the same politics and a love of books.

One weekend in high school, Joan called and asked to come over. "I need to talk to you—and your parents. I'm so confused."

We went into my bedroom. "Close the door," she said. "I want to talk to you first.

"My parents sat me and my brother and sister down last night and said they had something to tell us, something they'd waited to tell us until we were old enough to understand. But I don't understand at all.

"They told us they have an open marriage."

"What's that?"

"My mother said it means she agreed my father could sleep with other women. I can't believe it. All these years. I thought they loved each other. I thought we had a close family. I'm completely confused. What does this mean about my family? How can I believe in them anymore?"

"Did they say how they feel about each other?"

"Yes. They said they love each other. My mother said this is all OK with her. I really want to talk to your parents. You have such a close family. I want to know what they think."

We sat with my parents in the living room. Joan was very matter of fact, not crying or angry when she told them. "I just want to understand how they can say they love each other if they have this kind of marriage."

Dad talked with Joan for a long time, in a frank, unemotional manner, the same way he talked about things with me when I was upset.

Joan had come to me before anyone else when she needed help. She'd revealed a terrible and private family secret. Sometime that year, I told her the story of my mother's escape.

When we met as adults, Joan said to my husband, "During high school, Ingrid told me the story of her mother's escape. I was so flattered. I knew she didn't talk about that with many people." She should have known what I kept secret from her.

MY SECRECY ADDICTION followed me into adulthood, my ability to appear engaged while revealing nothing personal. After college I taught at a private school in Dallas. Through a mutual friend, I met Anna, a teacher at the nearby high school. Her parents were Belgian.

We shared stories about looking like European girls during elementary school. We discussed teaching, politics, and books. Anna suggested we have breakfast together before work every Friday morning. She found a place that served waffles and strawberries.

I WAS SPREADING SLICED strawberries across the top of my waffle when Anna took a sip of her coffee and said, "I have something to tell you."

Her tone made me look up. "I'm not telling anyone else, not even my parents.

"I met a man last Saturday night. We stayed up all night talking. We've talked on the phone every night since then."

They'd met at the coffee urn during a high school debate tournament down in Austin. She was a coach for the debate team at the high school where she taught. He was a lawyer in Austin and helped as a coach for an Austin high school debate team.

I tried to cut pieces of waffle without looking away from her face as she talked. She took occasional sips of coffee, but her waffle lay on her plate.

"Craig asked me to have dinner with him that night, and after dinner we went to a coffee house." They'd listened to folk music and stayed there all night talking. They had breakfast together before her team's bus left for Dallas Sunday morning.

"He wants to come up here next weekend. What do you think? Can I really know enough about him to trust him after just one week? Enough to let him sleep on the couch in my apartment? I told him we had to know each other at least one month before we see each other alone like that. What do you think?"

Anna was telling me something she didn't plan to tell anyone else.

The entire time she talked, I wondered, *How can you confide this way in me when I would never confide in you? Don't you know that?*

A whole year later, she had confided every step of her relationship with him. I had helped her move into a bigger apartment. I had kept her engagement secret until she and Craig decided to announce it.

Sometime during that year, I decided to apply to law school. Studying for the LSAT and filling out applications consumed most of my free time, but I never mentioned what I was doing to anyone except my parents and Moms.

When I was accepted to law school, I told Anna.

"I always wanted to go to graduate school, but I decided to get married and have children instead," she said.

She talked to me only once after that. She and Craig invited themselves to my apartment for coffee one Friday evening. He sat in my living room and read off a handwritten list of reasons not to attend law school.

"I asked Craig to write this for you," Anna said. "As a lawyer, he understands how awful it is being one."

Craig went to law school, and he's telling me not to go!? I thought. But out loud I said, "Well, I'm going to law school anyway."

I guessed Anna was jealous because she'd given up her dream of graduate school. It didn't occur to me she could have been hurt and angry because I hadn't confided in her.

16

THE MOST EXCITING EVENT IN OUR FAMILY WAS MY BROTHER'S birth a month before my fourteenth birthday. Within hours, Dad snuck me past the nurses' station into Mom's hospital room so I could see that shriveled little baby wrapped in a blanket.

"He's so cute!" I said.

"Cute?" Dad laughed. "He's all shriveled up. Give him time." Dad prided himself on "saying it like it is," as he put it.

In a year's time, Neill could walk and talk enough to call me Wee Wee and to develop his favorite game with me. "Way uh, Wee Wee!" he'd demand far too early on Saturday mornings, as he piled his stuffed animals on my head. This did wake me up, but I laughed and hugged him, though I'd gone to bed at one or two in the morning. On days my mother picked me up from high school, she let Neill run up the hill toward me, yelling, "Wee Wee" in front of the other kids. I laughed and swooped him into a hug.

I went to college a year before Neill started kindergarten. We both grew up as only children, but we wrote to each other. Through the years, his letters shared his activities at camp, at Tante Nannie and Uncle Hal's, at Tante Sonja and Uncle Rob's, and at college. Mine shared trips to Taiwan and Japan, and life in law school.

We had adventures together, too. After my college graduation in western Massachusetts, our family stopped in Harvard Square on our way to the Cape. I took my six-year-old brother off alone, bought him *Charlie and the Chocolate Factory* and a triple decker strawberry ice cream cone. The three pink scoops immediately hit the sidewalk. I called it the Strawberry Splashdown and bought him another.

I took my brother into New York City from Tante Nannie and Uncle Hal's house when he was nine or ten. We went to the office of *Mad Magazine* where I introduced Neill to the receptionist as an avid fan from Dallas and asked if he could meet their staff. The artists and writers we'd both been reading for years invited us in and showed us the drawings they were working on.

When I taught in Dallas, I took eleven year old Neill to the movie theater near our house with a grocery bag full of homemade popcorn. We sat through an all-day showing of James Bond movies.

I never mentioned my father to Neill. I was afraid he'd look down on me.

17

MY FATHER AND DOTTIE CAME TO DALLAS IN THE SUMMER AFTER we moved there, the summer Neill was born, the summer before I started ninth grade. They didn't come alone.

Again, my father was by himself in the car when he picked me up first day. "I have some news, Sweetheart," he said. "Dottie and I have a foster son. His name is George."

In the face of my usual silence, he explained that George and his brother couldn't live with their parents anymore, so my father and Dottie asked George to live with them. They hoped to adopt him.

"His brother went to live with another family. We've met them. We drove to the town where they live. They're very nice people."

Dottie and George were waiting for us at the hotel.

I didn't respond.

The hotel was a tall, gray building with gray stone curlicues at the top. An elevator in the lobby took us to a narrow hallway where my father knocked on a door.

"We-e-ell, Ingrid," Dottie greeted me. She smiled and stepped aside to let us enter.

A boy a few years younger than I sat on a couch. He looked over at all of us.

"Ingrid," my father said. "This is George, our wonderful son."

George wandered over. He had a square, freckled face and brown hair in a crew cut. He wore a short sleeved red and white checkered shirt and jeans. He seemed to me like someone who'd grown up outside a city, without much education, and no interest in books—which didn't matter because the real Ingrid was only watching.

"Hi," I heard him say.

"Hello," I said, looking at the carpet to signal my distance.

We stood in a big room near two bulky padded chairs covered in fuzzy green material and a shiny, brown couch where George had been sitting. At the other end of the room, a dining table and chairs stood beside a stove, sink, and refrigerator. Down a short hall, I would later discover a bathroom and a view of a bedroom beyond.

A trip to the hotel pool began the afternoon activities. This time, my father wore a swim suit and carried an inflated beach ball. Dottie wore a swimsuit under a triangular shaped cover-up, blue with a yellow flower print. Silently, we took the elevator to the lobby, exited the hotel and walked to the fenced enclosure where concrete surrounded a rectangular pool.

As usual, I carried my book into the pool and stood in a corner. I stared at the book, but I saw George jump into the pool with a big splash, the ball in his arms. Dottie and my father eased themselves into the water.

"Toss me the ball, George," I heard my father say. I heard him catch it, and I heard Dottie chuckle, "Heh, Heh, you almost missed that one."

"Ingrid, don't you want to join us?" Dottie called to me.

"No."

Eventually, Dottie left to cook dinner, and my father sat in a chair beside the pool.

George carried the ball over to my corner of the pool. "Don't cha wanna play ball?" he asked. He threw it at me.

I reached my book out onto a dry spot beyond the pool's edge and went through the motions of playing catch for a few minutes. I tried to look away so he couldn't throw the ball to me, but he did anyway.

"I really want to read," I said.

"O.K."

George splashed around the pool by himself.

As soon as we settled into our chairs at the table, my father began with, "Let us say grace." No holding hands like in Crawfordsville, just the prayer that he and Dottie pronounced distinctly and George mumbled as if he hadn't quite learned it. "In Jesus' name. Amen," they ended. I stared at the empty plate in front of me.

We sat silently, eating the meatloaf, little round potatoes, and green beans Dottie brought to the table. She dished out vanilla ice cream for dessert. Throughout the meal, I stared at my plate and waited for the magic words.

"Well, Ingrid, it's time to take you back," my father said. "Dottie and George will stay here to clean up."

"I THINK IT'S TERRIBLE, separating brothers like that," my mother said. "In two different families, and not even in the same city. They'll never see each other."

I'd informed my parents about George and repeated what my father said about visiting George's brother.

Having George around made it easier for me because it gave my father and Dottie someone else to focus on. And I'd made my role clear to him: I read.

ONLY ONE MEMORABLE INCIDENT occurred after George joined their visits.

It was the summer before my senior year of high school. I was in the car alone with my father. He'd probably just picked me up. Not far from our house, he asked, "What name do you use in school?"

"Ingrid Roth."

"Not Ingrid Tyler?! Do your friends know I'm your father?"

"No."

He turned the car around and drove to my school. Summer school students drifted up the long sloping lawn toward their afternoon classes.

"Is this your school?"

"Yes."

"I'm going to tell your principal what your real name is. I'm going to tell your principal I'm your father. Get out of the car. We're going in to talk to your principal."

For some reason, I did get out of the car. Maybe to stop him.

"Please don't tell my principal!" I begged.

"You're coming with me," he shouted. He picked me up and threw me over his shoulder. It was the early 1960's. I wore a full skirt, but it didn't occur to me to wonder if my skirt was hiked up and my underwear showed.

My divided world was coming together. The two pieces weren't supposed to touch.

"Please! Please!" I begged. "Don't tell my principal. Please!"

There must have been such anguish in my voice that he stopped walking and put me down.

"Get into the car," he instructed.

He didn't mention the subject again.

That evening, when he dropped me off, I described everything to my parents, the question that sparked the incident, his driving me to the school, his throwing me over his shoulder to haul me to the principal, and my begging him to stop. I did not mention my anguish at the threat of the two separate worlds coming together.

"Don't worry about him," Dad said. "He's crazy. Really. We've known that. He's *meshuga*." As usual, Dad used the Yiddish word for crazy.

He said this as if it were a fact my parents had always known about my father but had held off telling me.

This pronouncement was supposed to make me feel better about the incident. It made me feel much worse about myself. I knew enough about genetics to understand that not only was I part Shvantz, but I had a crazy streak, too.

THAT WAS HIS LAST VISIT, right before my seventeenth birthday—before my senior year of high school. No one told me he wouldn't visit again. When he didn't show up during Christmas vacation senior year, I didn't give it much thought.

I was relieved to have him out of my life.

18

I DECIDED TO ATTEND LAW SCHOOL IN D.C., NEAR TANTE SONJA, Uncle Rob, and Moms, in Arlington, Virginia. I was thirty-two.

October of second year, I went to a Hillel hoping to meet a man. This Jewish college students' group was holding a folk music concert. The kind of people I felt comfortable with were likely to be there. The first person I saw in that auditorium was a man with dark brown hair and beard and a face that felt familiar. He stood right inside the entrance, his back against the wall, facing the rows of still empty folding chairs and the silent stage. I walked straight over to him, and he looked at me with deep brown eyes.

"You can tell how intelligent a person is from looking into their eyes," my mother told me when I was six or seven. Those eyes made this man the smartest person I'd ever met. And they held a kindness that made me feel secure. This attractive man was not manipulative. Within minutes, we were talking about his recent trip to China and my majoring in Chinese studies. His descriptions of what he'd seen in China—the clay soldiers, the craggy, gray mountains, the innumerable Buddhas—mixed with my descriptions of the porcelains I'd examined for hours in the museum during my summer in Taipei, the open markets, and the turquoise butterflies bright against the gray stone in Taroko Gorge.

"Ching Dynasty buildings and art, in general, are way too elaborate," he said at one point.

"*Ongepotchket*," I affirmed, using the Yiddish word for fussiness to confirm our agreement on the subject and to test for his recognition of the word. He gave me a quizzical look and failed the test.

I threw out another. "Do you work?"

"I'm a lawyer."

He wasn't a student! Next test. "How long have you worked?"

"Seven years."

He was the right age, not ten years younger than I was, like all the guys in my law school classes.

We stood at the back of the room and talked through the entire concert, barely noticing that people had filled all the chairs and groups playing guitars, tambourines, flutes, and fiddles passed on and off the stage.

The next day, as I walked over the wet sidewalks and yellow leaves on campus, I knew we'd continue to talk. He called me every night.

A WEEK LATER, we sat in a West African restaurant where the dark oranges and rich browns of batiks warmed the walls. A candle in a glass globe lit the space on the tiny table between us. Dwayne and I faced each other over spicy food and plunged into every topic we could stuff into one evening—foods we liked, favorite hikes, our politics now and whether we'd been against the war in Vietnam during college, what we had thought about the radical groups roaming around our campuses, that we hadn't joined the dope smoking groups on campus because we hated losing control of our brains, that both of our families discussed politics and debated issues at meals, that Dwayne was a member of N.O.W. and his mother had helped start a chapter in Detroit, that both of us were Reform Jews and cared about being Jewish, my mother's escape— every discussion with me in those days came down to my mother's escape— and that we'd each traveled alone in Israel after college.

"I have to tell you one of the things I did there," Dwayne said.

Several topics earlier, we'd finished eating, and he'd reached across the table to hold my hand.

"You know the *Hasidim* approach Jewish men on the street in Jerusalem?"

"Yes. I saw them doing it." These ultra-Orthodox men who called themselves the pious ones—*Hasidim*—were known for sidling up to Jewish men on the streets to teach them the true way to be Jewish.

"Well, it happened to me after I'd been there a few days. Two men in fur covered hats and long black coats invited me to one of their homes for lunch. I knew they wanted to 'convert' me into a *Hasid*. The fact is, I was very interested in their understanding of what it is to be Jewish. So, I spent a few days with them. But I had no intention of being converted. I prayed with them and learned to wrap *tefillin*."

My mother had told me her father wrapped those black boxes and straps onto his forehead and arm during the Morning Prayer. The boxes, Dwayne explained, contain texts from the *Torah*, telling us to remember that God saved us when we were slaves in Egypt, that we must teach this to our children, that we must love and fear the one God and carry out his commandments.

"I studied with them and ate with them. They asked me to move in with them, but I refused. I'd rented a room in the Old City, and I knew I had to go back to my own room every night—to keep my perspective. When they weren't praying, they were discussing Talmud and how it applied to everyday problems. They had a big argument that went on for hours about whether you could turn off a light on *Shabbat* once it was accidently turned on. They were very nice to me, but I can't live the way they do. I can't spend my life debating whether or not to turn off a light."

I was impressed by Dwayne's desire to learn from these *Hasidim* and his interest in exploring a different approach to Judaism. Maybe most of all I was struck with his decision to keep his perspective by maintaining a room of his own. He formed opinions carefully and protected himself.

THE FOLLOWING SATURDAY, Dwayne picked me up in the morning. He'd suggested we shop for ingredients and cook dinner for that night, unlike the men who'd taken me to fancy restaurants on K Street or brought me roses—date by number, with corresponding conversation.

"I'm taking you to Eastern Market," Dwayne said when he started the car. "It's my favorite place to grocery shop. If you're interested in spaghetti, I know exactly where we should go."

"I love spaghetti."

We parked and walked around the corner into a landscape of stalls and tightly packed stores.

"I've been coming here ever since I moved to Washington. It reminds me of the North End in Boston where I did my grocery shopping in law school."

His hand slipped over mine, his long thin fingers winding around my much smaller hand.

"Here's where I buy Italian food."

We climbed up a steep doorstep into a long, narrow shop with shelves packed from ceiling to floor along one wall.

"I make spaghetti sauce with sausage. Is that alright with you?" Dwayne asked.

"It's fine. It sounds interesting."

Dwayne took me straight to a counter at the back of the store where he ordered several long strands of sausage and blocks of Parmesan and Romano.

"One more thing in here."

I followed him to a section of the wall lined with boxes of pasta.

"Do you want angel hair or thicker noodles?" Dwayne asked.

"I'd like angel hair, but what do you want?" Dwayne reached for a box of angel hair.

Outside, I zipped my coat up to my neck despite the sunniness of the late October morning.

"And now," Dwayne announced. "*T'maytas.*"

"You Detroiters say *t'maytas*!?" I laughed. "I say *tomaTOES.*"

"You Texans don't know how to talk." He grinned.

We wandered through the stalls until we found a pile of deep, red tomatoes.

"These will be much better than canned," Dwayne said.

"Look at that stall over there." I pointed. "Those are the biggest pumpkins I've ever seen."

"Oh! Pumpkin pie is my favorite. You said you can bake. Let's buy one and make a pumpkin pie."

"I've never made a pie from a fresh pumpkin before, only canned."

"We'll figure it out. I'm buying this pumpkin."

"O.K. We'll figure it out."

On the drive back, I discovered Dwayne had his mother's old *Joy of Cooking*, the cookbook I used for making pumpkin pie.

We carried our packages up two flights of worn wooden stairs to Dwayne's top floor apartment—one of four apartments that had resulted from the division of an old house a few blocks north of Dupont Circle. I placed my packages on the counter between the tiny kitchen and the living-dining room and looked around me.

Furnished with Scandinavian teak tables and leather padded chairs set among woven wall hangings, the long living-dining room extended along the kitchen to a bay of tall windows that provided a view of the street below and made me feel I was in a tower.

"The sausage is what makes the spaghetti special," Dwayne proclaimed from the kitchen. I watched him push the stuffing out of the sausage wrapper into an enormous pot where the meat sizzled and filled the air with its spices while he stirred. I grated the

Parmesan and Romano. He added the tomatoes, poured in red wine, and put a lid on the pot.

At the counter between the kitchen and living-dining room, I searched through the *Joy of Cooking* for the pumpkin pie recipe. Dwayne looked over my shoulder.

"Brandy! This recipe calls for brandy," he said. "That sounds great."

"We don't have to put it in. I hate to waste your brandy."

"That's what it's for—to enjoy."

Together we halved the pumpkin, scraped out the seeds, put the pumpkin halves face down on a cookie sheet, and stuck it into the oven.

We cooked in the glow of Dwayne's small kitchen, pressing pumpkin pulp through a sieve, rolling pie dough, simmering and tasting the sausage and tomato sauce. We listened to James Taylor, Gordon Lightfoot, and Joni Mitchell, the smells of cinnamon, nutmeg, freshly grated ginger, oregano and basil insulating us from the brittle cold of the street below.

At dusk, we sat side by side at Dwayne's table in the tower part of the room. He poured a dark red wine, and we ate the meal we'd created.

19

"HE'S THE ONE FOR YOU."

I'd invited Dwayne to a dinner party at Tante Sonja and Uncle Rob's house within weeks after we met.

Moms, in her medium high heels and a beige wool dress, walked toward me to make this pronouncement as I stood alone filling my plate from the buffet dinner on Tante Sonja's dining room table.

"I know, Moms," I said with no effort to hide my irritation at being told what to think. I didn't realize then I'd repeat that statement of her approval the rest of my life, like fingering an inherited jewel that hung at my neck from a gold chain.

MOMS AND TANTE SONJA championed Dwayne while my mother urged me in every phone call to date other men. If he hadn't mentioned marriage yet, she claimed after the first three months we were dating, he was already married and just "playing around" with me.

"DON'T LISTEN TO YOUR MOTHER." Moms was adamant.

Tante Sonja in a chair beside Mom's hospital bed agreed.

"You've dated enough men," Moms continued. "It's time you learned how to have a relationship."

I'd taken time off from studying to visit Moms in the hospital. Tante Sonja said she'd only be in for a few days for something Tante Sonja referred to as a minor procedure.

The next time I drove over to see Moms she was asleep in her bed at home. Tante Sonja had left the door unlocked so I could visit Moms while Tante Sonja and Uncle Rob were at work. I was afraid to wake Moms.

The last time I drove over, she lay asleep in a hospital bed as I stood, silent, beside her. Her face was blotched with big brown spots. She died that afternoon.

SPONGE CAKE. I'D NEVER liked that dry, airy stuff. The afternoon of Moms' funeral, it was the only thing I could eat—and only one piece. I could barely see the plates of lox, herring, cheeses, bagels, dark bread, salads, and noodle kugels friends had thrust onto Tante Sonja's dining room table. Within twenty-four hours of Moms' death, we had all gathered at Tante Sonja and Uncle Rob's house, the three *tantes* (including my mother), and the cousins, except Nancy and Rachel who had moved to Israel. The out of towners stayed at the house. I drove over first thing every morning, all seven days we sat *shiva*. I needed to be with the family. Dwayne came with me. We'd been dating over a year.

Almost as soon as we'd returned from the funeral, Lenny and Daniel brought out old photographs taken before the War and during the escape. In the front sitting room, they stacked piles of the small black and white pictures on several of the TV tables Tante Sonja had scattered through the house for people to eat on. In that room, where a low table along the front window held silver and gold framed pictures of the family's life in America, a dark wood grandfather clock flanked a fireplace, and a lace covered table stood between a cushy brown sofa and matching armchair, I watched Daniel leaf through the pictures and interview Uncle Rob about the escape while Lenny taped his answers. Dwayne leaned forward in a folding chair he'd carried into the room—absorbing everything.

At the back of the house, in the long living-dining room, a breakfront displayed the silver bowls, porcelains, and crystal Tante Sonja and Uncle Rob had collected on trips back to Europe in recent years, and plush white couches surrounded a low glass coffee table near a picture window. There, the rest of the family congregated and reminisced about things they could bear to discuss.

The family that wouldn't exist if Moms hadn't saved us. The family in which every *tante* and uncle was an interchangeable parent for the cousins, and the cousins felt like siblings. I felt that strength all around me and wanted Dwayne to be witness—and be part of it.

What I needed to do was unmistakable. I whispered to Dwayne, "Let's go for a walk. I have to tell you something terrible about myself."

We pulled our jackets around us as we closed the front door, headed down the concrete steps beside the azalea bushes Moms had planted years before, and continued over the short concrete walk between the two small rectangles of lawn still withered from the winter. We'd barely reached the main sidewalk when I blurted, "Dad is not my real father. My mother divorced my real father when I was a baby. I've been keeping this a secret all my life. My parents asked me to. You're the first person I've ever told. I thought you should know about my family—about the divorce."

Dwayne was the first person I'd ever wanted to tell, since that one girl in first grade.

His reaction was immediate. He looked at me and laughed. "Is that all? My grandmother was divorced. She was a lawyer in Detroit and raised two sons alone."

It wasn't relief or amazement that struck me, but the realization that I was not condemned. The first step toward shedding my Shvantzness and my crazy streak. The first step toward accepting myself.

We walked for blocks past the red brick houses and small rectangular lawns in that Arlington neighborhood. Dwayne told me his grandmother was one of the first female students in her law school. Dwayne's father and uncle remembered her studying in the bathtub when they were small boys. She had her young sons serve subpoenas on unsuspecting people once she became a lawyer. I told him my father wasn't Jewish and that I hadn't seen him for years.

When we returned from an hour or two in the neighborhood, I'd become closer to Dwayne than to anyone else—ever.

20

DURING THE LAST SEMESTER OF LAW SCHOOL, MY MOTHER forwarded a sealed letter from a lawyer in Crawfordsville, Indiana. He wrote that Aunt Kanka had died and left me a painting of my great grandmother. He asked where the painting should be sent and stated he was a lifelong friend of Aunt Kanka.

My father and I hadn't been in touch for seventeen years.

A third year law student, I understood that his visitation rights had expired when he'd stopped coming and that my mother had no obligation to allow him to see or talk to me. I'd been relieved when those visits ended and never asked why.

Dwayne and I discussed the letter that evening over dinner in his apartment. We sat at the teak dinner table in the tower part of the room. Dwayne always set our placemats next to each other so we sat close, our backs to the window, facing the room where, now, a golden light from the lamps spread over the dark browns of the teak and leather furniture.

"I want the painting, I but I don't want my father to find me through this lawyer." I stared at the chicken and chickpea stew on my plate.

"You should meet him. Not right away, but when you're ready."

Dwayne suggested I could tell the lawyer the situation and ask if he'd be a point of contact between me and my father without revealing my address or phone number.

This felt right to me, but I was terrified. "How can I do that to my parents? And how can I face that man?"

"You have to, eventually," Dwayne urged. "You need to learn about your family—and yourself.

"I'll be with you," Dwayne promised.

I called the lawyer the next day, summarized the secrecy and my fear. I would need to decide if I could be in touch with my father, I explained. I did want to learn more about my family and might soon be ready to contact my other aunts. The lawyer told me Aunt Mary Frances had died a few years before Aunt Kanka. Aunt Lippy lived near me, in Silver Spring, Maryland. He'd send me her address.

THE FIRST CONTACT OCCURRED eight months after the lawyer's letter arrived. One afternoon after bar review classes, an envelope with the lawyer's return address lay in my mailbox.

I carried the unopened envelope up in the elevator and down the dimly lit hallway to my fourth floor apartment—a stark studio apartment with a parquet floor stretching from the entrance to a far wall of metal edged windows that cranked open. A square walnut colored table and clunky matching chairs—the landlord's only contribution to the furnishings—stood beside the kitchen appliances and sink lined up along one wall. Across from the kitchen, I'd added a twin-sized couch bed and a long Masonite table with a brown metal frame. I'd spent hours at that table during law school, my back to the room, pouring over law books, outlining cases, pounding out papers on my portable typewriter—and, now, the summer after graduation—studying bar review materials. On Wednesday evenings, Dwayne shared whatever dinners I managed to prepare.

I stood inside the door of that apartment and slit open the envelope from Crawfordsville. *Your father asked me to forward this birthday card to you* the lawyer had written on his office stationery. I pulled out a small envelope and opened it to discover a card with a picture of a rabbit that looked like an illustration from my childhood fairytale books.

My father had filled every page of the card and both sides of a separate piece of paper. He wrote that he'd tried to call me on my birthday but couldn't reach me. He said he'd been with me the day before my sixth birthday that August in Houston and he had told me he wouldn't be with me on my birthday but would think of me. He wrote that I had responded, "*I'll be thinking of you all my life, whether I see you or not.*" He wrote that this was a quote from his notebook of my "sayings", this one dated the day before my sixth birthday.

My sixth birthday was my first birthday in Houston. That would have been his first trip to Houston. But his first visit I remembered—when my mother began calling him The Shvantz— must have been in December of that year. I couldn't imagine myself having said such a thing to him in Houston. They were the words of a guileless little girl to a Daddy she loved and felt completely comfortable with. What I would learn years later helped me understand that quote.

He also wrote that he always thinks of me on my birthday, and all other days and prays for God to bless me and fill me *with His Holy Spirit*. Those somber words chilled me with their unfamiliarity.

Ingrid, he continued, *I don't know why there has been an atmosphere of concealment of truth about your father, in your household, with the tenseness and fear that is bound to result from such action. Certainly it is not unusual for a divorced person to have a child by a first and second marriage and live in the sweet freedom that openness brings.* Near the end, he said when he'd recently called the house in Dallas to wish me happy birthday, he'd spoken to my *half-brother.*

The words on the card in my hand blurred as I tried to absorb them. He was clearly criticizing my parents for hiding his relationship to me from my school and friends, for cordoning him off from my life as much as possible. And his use of the term "half-brother"—a term foreign to our family—was his way of laying claim to me.

Did openness bring "sweet freedom," I wondered. The statement made openness sound so tempting. If only we'd been open about the strands of my family, we would have felt such freedom—whatever exactly freedom meant. Was it really that simple? What was "sweet" about my openness to Dwayne when I revealed The Secret in that walk outside Tante Sonja and Uncle

Rob's house was his acceptance—not a certainty until I heard it, though not a complete surprise, based on what I already knew about him. It was Dwayne's acceptance that brought freedom—to be recognized for who I am by someone important to me.

My father was writing in 1982 that it wasn't unusual for people to have children by more than one marriage. I thought about my mother's fear of condemnation for being a divorcee in the Ozzie and Harriet world of the 1950's and early '60's. I thought about how hard it may have been for Dwayne's grandmother, a divorcee in the 1920's, who had no choice about being open—because she was a single parent. She had to stand proudly with her sons by her side, for all of their sakes. That took courage. Would my mother have done that if she hadn't remarried and moved across the country?

I remembered the question from one of my teaching colleagues in the private boys' school in Dallas when we teachers were eating lunch in the school cafeteria and discussing the growing number of divorces in the country in the 1970's. "Look around you," he said to the rest of us. "How many students do you see from broken homes?" We looked at our upper middle class student body eating and chattering in that private school cafeteria. We knew the families of those students for whom we'd each been an "advisor," and we were incredulous when we focused on the high number with divorced parents. Even in the mid-1970's, when divorce was commonplace, he'd used the disapproving term "broken homes," and none of us had challenged it.

After teaching that day, I'd returned to my apartment, curled up on the couch with a mug of tea, and called my mother. My brother attended that private school. I knew she'd be interested in that lunchroom conversation and the teachers' surprise at the high divorce rate among the families who sent their kids there.

"I'm glad Dad and I didn't raise you and Neill with a broken home." Mom had said. "We have a perfect family."

"We do," I'd replied.

During that cafeteria conversation, it hadn't occurred to me that I came from a divorced family. The parents who raised me loved each other.

I returned from my reflections to my apartment in D.C. where I looked down at my father's birthday card still in my hand. I slipped the card into the envelope with the lawyer's note and filed this with the lawyer's other correspondence. I wasn't ready to contact my father. But the poignancy of the lost relationship between that guileless girl and her Daddy lingered.

A few days later, a postcard arrived from Dad. He and Mom were in Venice. Dad's dark humor and keen political insight provided a distraction.

We are sitting in the Palazzo Grassi which has an exhibition of Modigliani's etchings. We have already seen the Doge's Palace and formed our opinions about the kind of men who ruled the Venice city state. They appreciated life-like art and were quite capable of cruelty, murder, and torture at the same time. The form of their palaces was always made with the preoccupation of defense of their own lives.

21

NEWLY GRADUATED FROM LAW SCHOOL, WITH THE BAR EXAM
barely behind me, I started work for a tax law journal and began
night classes to earn a master's in tax law.

In the midst of these changes, I stood under the *chupah* with the
only man I'd ever wanted to meet under a marriage canopy.

And I set out trying to give myself permission to defy my
parents and contact my father. I carried around yellow legal pads
and stopped in the middle of meals, in parking lots before I turned
on the car engine, on street corners waiting to enter the cross walk,
to jot down the thoughts that rushed through my mind.

A YEAR AFTER RECEIVING the birthday card, I wrote to my father.
What to call him was an issue. I had avoided addressing him at all
after he became The Shvantz—unless I was asking for something. I
sure didn't want to call him "Dad" or "Daddy" now. That letter
went through as many drafts as a law school paper, and I asked

Dwayne to read and mark suggested changes on my final draft before I typed it. I kept a copy.

October 15, 1983

Dear Father,

Because we haven't been in contact for so many years, it was extremely difficult for me to decide to write this letter. However, I want to know how you are and to tell you about me. It is also very important for me to learn more about my childhood and your family.

You can probably understand why I have been afraid to write to you. It is only after much thought and agonizing that I have overcome enough of my fear to write you now. The circumstances of our relationship made your visits terribly uncomfortable for me. I have been made to feel that a conflict exists between my two families which renders their mutual participation in my life impossible. I am very close to my parents and brother, don't want any interference with that closeness, and won't permit any interference. Finally, I still fear being fought over.

Please understand that I do not know how much contact my emotions can accommodate. Therefore, I must communicate with you at my own pace, confining our communication to letters, initially. I hope this is amenable to you.

I remember your teaching me about fireflies and snapping turtles, and your taking me to a place where we pumped water from a spring. I remember our fishing trip when I was afraid of the dragonflies. You showed me

Crawfordsville, a town of white clapboard houses and porch swings.

Maybe our outings explain why I now like camping and hiking so much.

But I constantly flee from the happy memories to my fears of the strangeness. Then, I remember your sitting in a motel room reading to me out of the New Testament, even though you knew I was Jewish. I resented this proselytizing and your failure to accept and address my Jewishness.

Being Jewish has formed a large part of my identity. The holidays with the honey cakes, candles, matzos, and songs were welcome celebrations. The ethics—such as remembering that we were once strangers in Egypt and, so, must accept and have compassion for the stranger—have been central to my behavior and belief. Being a Holocaust survivor's child has both plagued me with grief—I used to cry uncontrollably at a mention of the Holocaust—and provided me with my strongest sense of direction: Because I know about the evil even highly scientific, modern man is capable of perpetrating, I must ensure that such genocide, or other atrocities, will not happen again, to anyone. My knowledge of my grandmother's strength and brilliance in saving her family has made me proud and anxious to be as capable. I do not consider myself a religious Jew, though I respect people who are religious—in any faith. What I respect most is ethical and kind behavior.

Here, I summarized my education and travels and told him of my marriage the year before, describing Dwayne as the most open-minded and kind man I'd ever met. I enclosed a picture from our wedding. I also enclosed some of my poems to give him a concept of me. They were about the Holocaust and being Jewish.

Near the end, I stated, *You and I are extremely different in certain respects, but also may have much in common.* Dwayne had softened that sentence.

I closed with regards to Dottie, my hopes that they were both well, and a request that he tell me about his life, how he spent his time, and what their home was like. I signed my name—with nothing more.

Within a week, his reply arrived. Dwayne and I stood together at the kitchen counter in his apartment, where we both now lived. I opened the envelope and found pictures and a letter inside.

When I was in elementary school, my mother had once shown me a few of my baby pictures taken in a studio. Later, she had shown me one or two pictures of myself as a toddler, slices of pictures cut with a scissors so that the parts with my mother and me remained. The only other pictures I'd seen of my early childhood were pictures Tante Sonja had of me and Lenny in our overalls out behind the apartment.

I looked at the picture on top of the small pile my father had sent. A fat faced baby lay between layers of blankets in a bassinet and smiled at someone off to the side. *Ingrid Tyler* was penciled on the back of the photograph. I handed the picture to Dwayne and picked up another. A small girl squinted at the camera, her blonde hair pulled back with a barrette. A white collar covered the top of her dark plaid dress from her neck out to the short, puffy sleeves and down to her waist. Dwayne laughed.

In the next picture, the same girl leaned against the front bumper of a car. Her hands shoved into the pockets of a double breasted coat, her eyes bore into the camera with a stern look, her lips pursed menacingly between chipmunk cheeks. Defender of the car. Dwayne and I howled with laughter which increased when we saw the next picture. There was the girl, her face drawn down in a solemn expression beneath a white hat with a curled up brim. She wore a pale, waist length jacket over a short dress, white socks and patent Mary Janes on her feet. Baggy white gloves—maybe her mother's—covered her hands and arms which dangled at her sides. This must have been a church outfit.

My father had penciled a note on the back of the car picture: *You and our 1950 "Buick Special." Your mother once took you into downtown Washington from our apartment in Mt. Rainier, Md., by bus, and you said, "I like my new Buick Pecial better."*

I was seeing myself as part of that other family and that other life. I was seeing myself before my mother and I left.

The last picture was the only one in color. I looked into the faces of my father and Dottie—with gray hair. My father in a light gray jacket, white shirt, and red tie pinned (I now know) with the insignia from the Signal Corps, sat holding his guitar, hands positioned as if ready to play. Behind him, Dottie stood in a simple light blue dress with a round neck at her throat, and two long strands of pearly beads, one hand on my father's shoulder and one straight at her side. Both of them looked into the camera from behind eyeglasses, with dignified, but happy smiles, smiles that made me feel as if they couldn't wait to engage me in one of their songs. These were kind, open faces. I looked into those faces for a long time before I picked up the letter.

October 21, 1983

My Dearly Beloved daughter, Ingrid,

First, let me congratulate Dwayne and offer our warmest love and best wishes to you both, in your marriage. We're very grateful for the picture. It now graces our living room. We have added Dwayne to our prayers.

My Dear, it would be impossible for me to express my appreciation for your beautiful and thoughtful letter.

As I was putting on my hiking shoes this morning, preparing to walk in the light rain to my "communing grove" (a pine woods with much other colorful growth, where we saw blue birds fly down and get something from on top of the snow last winter) about a mile away, with Dottie, I thought about your letter. Your loving gesture of writing to me can change our lives, like being upheld by the hand of the Lord through his divine touch, if we are aware of the opportunity to offer, each to the other, the best of our understanding, love, and compassion. I'll pray to be helped to do this, on my part.

The night Dottie and I became engaged, I said it would be necessary for both of us to have love for your mother— meaning the kind of love indicated by the Greek word "agape."

In the many efforts I made to reach you again by telephone, during the present year, I've had loving conversations with both your mother and Bennie.

Ingrid, your wonderful letter arrived very late yesterday afternoon, and as soon as I simmered down I started making notes of things to tell you. I want to do a thorough job of answering your "questions," and commenting on your interesting information and observations. But I know you'll want to have an answer to your letter as soon as feasible, so I'll run this up to the post office and soon get started on a more detailed "story of my life," "et cetera, et cetera" (to quote from "Anna and the King of Siam."), to be mailed when I learn that this has been received.

We've started going through pictures we thought you'd like to have, and I'm enclosing a small batch.

Believe me, I understand very well about the emotional impact involved in your loving and thoughtful step, but we're very eager to share the beauty of western North Carolina with you two hikers. We really don't want to rush things, but if you should feel that about a two day visit might be feasible fairly soon, while the foliage is beautiful, please call us and know that you'll be welcome at "Tyler's Haven of Harmony."

There's a magnificent State park not far away, with a great mixture of majestic trees, including one of my favorites, the hemlock, and crystal clear mountain streams.

Dottie sends scads of love to you both.

With abiding love,

Dad

He'd included their phone number.

My father's statement about adding Dwayne to their prayers, his reference to Divine touch, his comment to Dottie about agape, and the mention of his communing grove—were all indications of a piety I'd never been exposed to.

And I could imagine the "loving conversations" with my parents when my father telephoned our home. I could hear Dad talking to my mother about the approach they should take whenever my father called, "Try to let me handle the calls, Sienie, so you have to be involved as little as possible. Above all, we must treat him with kid gloves—and get off the phone as quickly as possible. We don't need to have him going *meshuga* on us."

I could hear Mom on the phone with my father, saying a few sentences in her restrained but polite voice before, "Here's my husband, he'd like to talk with you, too," and Dad saying in his phony charming voice, "How are you Bill? I hope all's well."

But I focused on the kind faces in that photograph and the excitement of seeing Ingrid in that early life. The blue birds on the snow, and the trees and streams in the state park stayed with me.

22

WITHIN DAYS, I REPLIED. I TOLD HIM DWAYNE AND I OPENED HIS letter together. We looked at the picture of him and Dottie.

I have looked into your faces over and over again. You have such kind faces. I can't believe I tortured you with my silence.

And the other pictures made me very happy. How strange to see me at the time of my life that has become shrouded in secrecy.

We planned to visit in the future, I said. I would tell my parents and other relatives about reconnecting with him after we visited. I also told him I enjoyed hearing about his woods.

In his next two letters, my father began to tell me about himself. He described their "work"—he wrote songs, and he and Dottie sang them for organizations and events he listed on two pages. They included churches, patriotic events, the DAR, the Woodrow Wilson Birthplace Foundation, nursing homes, an apple blossom festival, a Stephen Foster memorial festival, public and private schools, a small town television show in South Carolina, and the Gideon Society—the very group that had kept his motel rooms stocked with the Bibles he read to me during Christmas vacations. They ranged geographically from Virginia to Illinois, Indiana, Florida, and North and South Carolina.

In seeking to do something at least on the positive side in our work, I've received great inspiration from the experience of Moses, whom God insisted He was going to use although Moses protested that he was incapable of carrying out the mission given him.

You may like to review Browning's "Pippa Passes" if it isn't fresh in your memory. It had a great influence on me as I prepared a longish "speech of persuasion" for a speech course in college. I was asked to present it at some churches. The talk was based on the dramatic effect that Pippa's little song of joy and faith had when heard by various people at a crucial time in their lives.

I've just begun to realize that this dramatic work of Browning's has probably played a key part in determining my calling. At least I'd like to think that my calling is consistent with the theme of "Pippa Passes."

He diverged to other subjects.

I could not possibly have anything but the warmest love for you, Ingrid, and I would be unable to carry on at all effectively in life if I permitted myself to have anything but love and compassion for all who have been concerned with your life. We all know that even some of the greatest "wrongdoers" have been used to do the most magnificent things for mankind—for instance Moses, who killed a man in anger, was used not only to set God's people free, but to bring His children His great laws, including "Thou shalt not kill."

I know from personal experience that it troubles us the most when we do not give honesty its proper place. I would like for all concerned in our relationship to feel only the peace and release that can come from fearlessly accepting things as they are. For my part, I would be grateful for forgiveness for anything I may ever have done, or failed to do, that resulted in any distress for you, Ingrid.

Including his daily routine.

I do almost invariably walk to "my" communing grove to get away from the world and receive specific inspiration and marching (or, often, "relaxing") orders from the highest Source. Afterwards, Dottie and I take time to have devotions—reading a page from a daily devotional booklet and the Scripture from references given there (sometimes from the Old Testament), repeating some Scripture of basic importance, praying, singing a hymn, and reading additional passages of the Old and New Testaments from various "versions." I try to get in additional walking by walking to our business district—one and a half or two miles round trip.

If I'm working on a new song, it's in my head all the time, virtually. Dottie can tell, at meals, when to say, "You're working, aren't you?" Writing and pacing off

> *rhythm can go on through a large part of the night, too. On*
> *the mountain, in Virginia, I once got in bed (possibly not*
> *for the first time that night), and said to Dottie, "I've*
> *finished the song. Do you want to hear it?" She not only*
> *agreed, very sleepily, but also very sleepily made a pertinent*
> *comment that led to an important change in the song.*
>
> *I do well to get in two hours' of guitar practice.*

They occasionally watched television in the evenings, especially the PBS nature programs, not "childish" shows. I learned that he had worked at the U.S. Public Health Service in the Division of Foreign Quarantine in D.C., part of the Health, Education, and Welfare Department. When his office moved to become part of the CDC in Atlanta in 1967, he retired early *(with a tiny annuity) because I wanted to be on my own.* They moved to a small town in Virginia, near Shenandoah National Park because they could buy a little house with one-third the property taxes they'd paid near D.C. From there, my father and Dottie moved to a small town in Florida, and eventually to the small town in North Carolina where they now lived. He didn't mention what George was doing.

He urged me to remember my sense of humor and not to be afraid of writing about happy subjects because I might think they're frivolous. He said he supported my legal career and praised my prior work with children as a teacher.

I absorbed every part of those two letters over the next few days.

My father's songs were nothing like my poems, but when I read his description of writing songs and of Dottie's recognition that he was writing a song, I remembered one of my fifth grade students saying, "Miss Roth, you must be writing a poem. You have that look on you." I taught poetry writing in my language arts classes, and told my students I wrote poems.

Again, he'd criticized my parents, as he had in his birthday card the year before, but this time more harshly. Anger rang through his comparison of my parents' actions to Moses' killing a man.

His daily routine was largely prayer, prayer, and more prayer. His letters barely mentioned any subject other than their religion, their work being an integral part. His comments about love and compassion for my parents, and giving honesty its proper place—especially in light of his apparent enduring anger—sounded like a person repeating what he'd learned in therapy—in his case, religious training after the divorce. What aspect of the divorce drove him to that?

During my teaching internship in Boston, a friend and I had watched *Hasidic* men dance in their synagogue. Like tourists, we stood in an alley outside the open door to a low ceilinged, dimly lit room where the ultra-Orthodox bearded men in wide black hats and long black coats danced in concentric circles, arms around each other's shoulders, stomping their feet and singing.

Reform Jewish men wore modern clothes and didn't dance in prayer. They read prayer books in pews among the women of the congregation. Precisely because it was so unfamiliar I had wanted to see that scene in the *Hasidic* synagogue. I would later travel to Taiwan and wander through the streets, absorbing things I'd never imagined. Rows of cooked ducks hanging from stalls. Families eating in those stalls—their bedding visible behind sheets of plastic—and washing their rice bowls in the open sewers that ran beside the streets.

I knew I needed to face the reality of who my father was: a pious, cloistered man. I knew I could do it, but I was afraid.

23

I WAS SETTING THE TABLE FOR DINNER, ONE OF THE CHORES THAT helped me earn my penny allowance at age eight.

"Look Inky. Look at this."

My mother stood at the other end of the table where she'd laid a pile of mail. She held up a black and white photograph the size of a piece of notebook paper. I walked over. A baby's face filled the photograph, a baby with a double chin and a pointed tuft of hair on its head.

"Do you know who this is?" my mother asked.

I looked more closely. *Henry* was handwritten in the bottom right hand corner.

"A baby named Henry."

My mother laughed. "No. It's you! Henry was the name of the photographer."

"That fat baby is me?"

"Yah. You were so cute. Here, you were about six months old."

"Not cute to me." I turned away to fold the napkins.

"I thought you were the cutest baby I'd ever seen."

I walked around the table to lay the cutlery at each of our places. My mother looked at me.

"I really like The Shvantz's sisters," she said, apparently out of nowhere. "They are good people and very smart. I still write to them every year to wish them merry Christmas." She picked up the mail she'd been looking at when she mentioned the picture.

The Shvantz made me write to my aunts on cards he handed me whenever he visited. After my mother said that about my aunts, I wrote *Love* above my signature and underlined it twice.

NOW AT AGE THIRTY-FIVE, for the first time since my trip to Crawfordsville, I would see Aunt Lippy.

I wrote her a letter. A week later, I called.

"Aunt Lippy, this is Ingrid."

"Oh, Ingrid. It's so good to hear your voice. I received your letter. You're living in Washington, right near me! And you're married! Oh, I can't wait to see you and meet Dwayne. And you're a lawyer!"

"Aunt Lippy, it's so good to hear your voice. You have no idea how excited I am. I can't wait to see you. We want you to come over for dinner. Tell me when you can come."

"Well, let's see now. It would be me and Bill. He lives with me, you know. How about Friday evening?"

"Wonderful! We'll meet you outside. The steps to our apartment building are steep and might be icy. We can help you."

On Friday evening, Dwayne and I peered out of our bedroom window down onto the street. I saw a car parking and a slim woman with gray perky hair step out of the driver's side. "There they are! They're getting out of their car. Quick! Let's go down."

We met them on the sidewalk below the steps where ice lay under the landlord's sand.

"Aunt Lippy!" I hugged her and hugged the man she introduced as Bill, a tall, wide man with a narrow ruff of white hair around his balding head and a plain, but open, face.

"Ingrid, I can't believe you're all grown up. The last time I saw you, you were four years old.

"I brought you a loaf of Irish soda bread from a bakery near our house." She handed me a plastic wrapped, hard, oval loaf.

I reached for her arm. "Let's climb the stairs together."

Dwayne asked Bill, "Can you make it?" To Bill's nod, he replied, "I'll be right behind you."

We sat around the long, teak table. Two tall white candles illuminated the blue straw placemats and blue rimmed plates. Dwayne served the Brunswick stew he'd taught me how to cook. He poured red wine. I sliced Aunt Lippy's bread and passed it around.

"I hope you like raisins in your Irish soda bread," Aunt Lippy said.

"I've never had Irish soda bread," I said, "but it looks thick and chewy—the way I like bread. And I love raisins."

Aunt Lippy, Dwayne, and I talked easily. Bill contributed an occasional comment. Aunt Lippy told us that she was seventy-two years old and she and Bill still folk danced once a week. "That's how we met." She smiled.

She told us Bill was a retired engineer, and Dwayne asked questions about Bill's work while I cleared the dishes before dessert.

"I made my favorite cake for you." I cut pieces of the cake swirled with apples, cinnamon, and pecans while Dwayne made tea.

"Oh, Ingrid, when you were a baby, I loved you so much I said I shouldn't have children of my own, because I'd never love them as much."

AUNT LIPPY AND I INITIATED weekly phone calls. She plunged straight into subjects other people might have hidden. I knew she'd been married to Uncle Tom, because I addressed both of them in the cards my father made me send. I wouldn't have raised the subject, but she did. Uncle Tom had died many years earlier, she told me. "He was an alcoholic and a smoker. I asked God to help him stop."

Aunt Lippy believed in God, but in a gentle, private way. "You're Jewish," was all she said about my religion and let me know she'd love to learn more about it from me. "If you wish."

"I was raised Methodist," she explained, "but every Sunday morning I go to the Catholic church Tom attended, because he was my husband. I don't believe in all they do."

Her openness made it easy for me to talk to her.

24

My father sent a short letter.

December 15, 1983

Dearest Ingrid,

This is just a brief follow-up note to say that when you and Dwayne visit us, you can be at ease about the thought that we would seek to have any "community" devotional period. Your visit will be our blessing.

I joined a law firm and continued my night classes in tax law. Letters flowed between me and my father.

He sent more pictures. The first set arrived one afternoon in early January. Dwayne and I stood at the kitchen counter with the pile of photographs. I picked up the first one.

August in St. Louis, my father had penciled on the back. That was right around my fifth birthday. Wearing a sundress, my hair in braids with bows at the top, I stood in front of my father and smiled happily into the camera. My father towered above me, in a dark sports jacket, shirt and tie, and light colored pants, his hands on my shoulders, a grin on his face.

I didn't remember his trip to St. Louis. But as I stared at that picture, I remembered two topics my parents had raised at dinner while we lived there: you're Jewish if you have a Jewish mother, and Dad's story about him and his friends being baptized repeatedly so they could get lollipops. My parents must have been planning for my father's visit. They were trying to preempt the possibility I'd believe him if he told me I was a Methodist because I was baptized as a Methodist.

A second picture was annotated, *In front of the house in Alexandria (where I kept the room with your youth bed and with nursery rhyme characters on the wall.)* My father and I stood side by side. I leaned against his leg, my head tilted toward him, a huge smile on my face. *I kept this little chair for you in the same house*, he'd written on a picture of me sitting in a little wooden chair, my face sparkling with happiness. This was the girl whose Daddy took her to special places on the weekends when she lived with Tante Sonja, Uncle Rob, Lenny, and Moms. She was probably four and a half.

In another batch of pictures a few days later, I saw me, maybe a year and a half, chin length blond hair pulled back by a barrette, seated on my father's shoulders, grinning. My father held my ankles. A stuffed animal's tail hung beside my father's face. He wore a dark double breasted suit and a proud smile.

Me, about the same age, with my father. In the foreground, our shoes and socks, side by side on the muddy bank of a stream. In the stream, my father stood in long trousers and a short sleeved shirt, holding me against his chest, our heads level. I looked down at the stream. He looked at me, seeming to appreciate my interest in the water.

My mother must have taken those two pictures.

A third installment. Among them a grinning barefooted girl in shorts and a T-shirt leaned against a tall man, her head barely above his waist, his arm around her, his hand resting on her shoulder. A light colored driving hat, one side slightly raised above a small rim, slanted across his head and shadowed his smiling face. My father had penciled, *Ingrid and Granddaddy in Crawfordsville. This is one of my very favorite pictures of you.* In another, my father and I stood side by side in front of the white porch of the Crawfordsville house, each of us extending an arm to hold three long fish that hung by their mouths from some kind of hook. There I was, the four year old who had gone to Crawfordsville with her Daddy. Those pictures keenly evoked my memories of that trip—the snapdragons, raspberry jam, water rushing over rocks, green moss, the dragonflies.

He sent a newspaper clipping from a Crawfordsville newspaper about his being commissioned as a second lieutenant and assigned to duty in the Army Signal Corps. The clipping contained a picture of him in uniform, his deep set eyes looking straight into the camera, his long narrow face serious and dignified beneath a military hat that was nearly overwhelmed by a shiny insignia with details undiscernible in the photograph.

He sent pictures of my mother who, in my memory, always had to wear the latest styles—even if she sewed all of her clothes. But in these pictures, she wore rolled up fishing trousers, a baggy shirt with rolled up sleeves, and a floppy canvas hat. Only her hair was stylish—for the late 1940's. The bangs were curled into a tight roll straight across her forehead, and the rest of her chin length dark hair flared like pyramids on both sides of her head. In one picture, she posed alone on a bridge with a fishing rod in her hand. In another, she crouched beside me seeming to teach me, barely one year old, how to hold the rod.

Annotated pictures continued to fill our mailbox. Me as a baby in my mother's arms. Toddler me with my mother, Aunt Lippy, Aunt Kanka, and Aunt Mary Frances. Me in Houston and in Dallas. Outside a motel room, in a swimming pool, being pulled in a cart by a pony, me with Kathy, the girl whose parents my father had befriended at the motel swimming pool, me with Dottie. Through the years, that girl with the unabashed smile changed into one who looked down at the ground or into the distance—and finally—into a teenager who stood beside her father—stone-faced.

During the weeks they arrived, I sank into those pictures and teetered on the brink of my two worlds, the one that was real and the secret one that didn't exist.

I POUNDED OVER THE SIDEWALK, my brown leather briefcase banging against my thigh, snow piled between me and the street, salt crunching under my boots. Past restaurant and shop windows. Past the bookstore where Dwayne and I sometimes ate brunch. Up the hill toward our apartment. Images and feelings propelled me. Over the green, peeling paint on the outside stairs, through the front door. Up the scuffed, wooden stairs to our door. I unlocked the bolt, threw myself into my desk chair, unlatched the brief case, pulled out my yellow legal pad, and scribbled:

Thanks to Dwayne—because he didn't reject me, but loved me, and saw the source of my problem—I have a father!

Who loved me and carried me and let me slosh my feet in the mud.

I know where I come from. He creates like me.

I was a baby. I hugged my Daddy's knees and sat on his shoulders and belonged to him and looked happy.

<u>My</u> *father. I love him.*

With my father, I smiled as we slipped off our shoes to wiggle our toes in the mud together. And after she took me away from him, I followed every stream to its source to find him.

But now I can laugh and smile and be silly because he'll protect me with fireflies in a jar at night. No Nazis will get me. We won't have furniture and Persian carpets that we can cry over losing. We'll stuff bags with pine needles to sleep on and curl up under big leaves or rocks to keep dry.

I love you Daddy. Dad. Father. Mine.

Why did she keep you from me for so long and Aunt Kanka from me forever?

You are not the monster. I was. How could I have hurt you?

I STOOD ON THE WOOD FLOOR of the entrance hallway inside our apartment where the big black phone sat on a narrow table beside the phone book. I held the receiver to my ear with my left hand and twisted the cord around the index finger of my right hand. Dwayne listened to me from the kitchen while he cleaned our Sunday brunch dishes.

"Mom, I feel like I can't discuss things with you."

"Ingrid, you know you can tell me anything. We're best friends."

"Mom, we've been on the phone for ten minutes, and all you've done is talk about your book club, and the friends you've been seeing. I care about those things, but you haven't said one word about my letter saying I've been in touch with my father and want to visit him—saying that I met Aunt Lippy. If only I could tell you whatever I want to, and you would listen to me. I've always listened to you. If only you would respond to what I wrote. It's as if my feelings mean nothing to you."

"Ingrid, I understand everything about you. You don't have to explain yourself to me."

I burst into tears, bent over the phone table, and sobbed into the phone until I could talk.

"You don't know all about me. I've been protecting you. I've hated myself for years because you hated my father and so did I."

"You didn't have to feel that way. They were an upstanding family."

"That's the first time you've ever said that."

"You don't need to feel this way about yourself. Adopted children don't know about their families. If you want to have a relationship with your family, go ahead.

"Dad and I talked about it when you were little. I could've seen your aunts and had fun with them. But I did not—for your sake. For your sake we kept them from you because we thought it would mix you up, since their lives are different from ours. I stayed in touch with them. You'll enjoy Aunt Lippy. He's narrow-minded. Aunt Kanka said so, too, six months before she died. Go ahead. Have a relationship with them. You can handle it."

My mother delivered this in her terse, business like, almost irritated tone. A tone of here's what I've decided to say. Let's not belabor the point.

"I can't talk any more right now, Ingrid," she finished. Her usual statement when she wanted no more discussion with me on a subject. I could imagine her head held high in her regal manner as she used this statement to end one of our mother-daughter conflicts and exit the room.

"INGRID, I WANT TO show you something."

Aunt Lippy stood up from her kitchen table where the two of us had eaten tuna salad sandwiches and tomato soup while Bill was off golfing and Dwayne was spending Sunday afternoon writing a brief. I followed her into the living room where two long branches studded with yellow flowers arced from opposite sides of a vase on her coffee table.

"I forced this forsythia to bloom."

She noticed the quizzical look on my face and explained that if you put the bare branches in water inside the warm house, the forsythia thinks it's spring time and blooms.

"I do this every winter."

"And now I have something else to share with you. Wait for me on the couch for a minute."

Aunt Lippy left the room and returned with books. She sat on a chair across from me, opened a notebook, and read me poems she'd written. Short rhyming poems about nature, God, and people she loved. They were not the kind of poetry I preferred, but her love for words was all that mattered. No one in my Dutch family weighed words and loved them.

"I want to read you some of Kanka's poems, too." Aunt Lippy opened a printed book and read words that formed hard edged emotions.

That day I learned where my poetry came from.

25

I WAS READY TO MEET MY FATHER. DWAYNE AND I WOULD FLY down to North Carolina early Saturday and fly back Sunday evening. After nineteen years, I was about to cross back into the world that didn't exist. And bring Dwayne with me. This would require travel into a land of Christian fundamentalism.

We could cross back into reality from the world that didn't exist. I had done that. But could we bring the two worlds together?

Minutes after we landed in North Carolina, Dwayne headed down the aisle of the small airplane, and I discovered a cliché was true. Knees really can feel like jelly when you're frightened. Determination carried me off that plane, down the stairs to the tarmac.

My father was hugging me—a tall man, bending over to pull me to his chest. And I was hugging the people with the kind faces in that picture.

"My dear daughter," my father said. "Dwayne you look just like your picture."

"Well, Ingrid—and Dwayne," said Dottie. "Did you have a good trip?"

"Let's get your suitcase into the trunk." My father opened the trunk, and Dwayne lowered the suitcase.

As we settled into the back seat of the car, my father began a monologue that would continue through the weekend. He began with logistics. It was an hour drive to their "little town." On the way, they were taking us to their favorite restaurant, and afterwards—as planned on the phone—for a walk in the state park. Very quickly, he slid into his primary subject. It was Jesus this and Jesus that, as we passed barns, cows, haystacks, flat faced wooden houses with small, square windows, and white trimmed brick houses peeking through trees. I looked out the window, but l listened. And I heard: "Jesus was a Jew." "Your Bible is our background."

INSIDE THE RESTAURANT, the cloth covered tables and small bud vases reminded me of where my father and I had eaten shrimp cocktail and fruit cocktail.

"This is my dear daughter, Ingrid. I haven't seen her for nineteen years," my father said to the hostess. "And my dear son-in-law, Dwayne. They've come to visit us from Washington, D.C."

Dwayne and I glanced at each other and looked away while my father grasped at this acknowledgement from the outside world that I was his daughter.

Over the bud vase at our table, my father's monologue continued as we ate, but the subject matter expanded. He told us they sang their songs at local public schools with funding from the county arts council. "The comments from students and teachers have been encouraging enough to help keep us going for as long as the Lord sees fit to use us."

He told us about his "wonderful inventions." The latest—in fast food restaurants, every table should have a hole at one end with a garbage container underneath so people could throw out their garbage right at the table.

He treated us to some of his puns. "Did you hear about the heavy set surgeon? He was a big operator.

"There was a detective who did such poor work that he hadn't pinned anything on anyone since his child was in diapers."

Dottie peppered his speech with her chuckles, "Heh, heh."

He recounted how he once found Aunt Lippy's run away dog. "It was a co-ink-ee-dink. That dog showed up on the same path in the woods where I took my morning walk." I silently recalled his use of that word from my childhood.

He spoke with the same exaggerated enunciation I remembered—like a self-conscious speech student. Unlike Dad's booming voice that radiated confidence and humor even before he headed off to bed in his baggy striped pajamas, "Goodnight, folks, you've had the pleasure of my company long enough!"

Dottie and I stood beside a rack of cards before we left the restaurant.

"Why look at those little critters." She pointed to a card with a drawing of rabbits in shirts and pants or flowery dresses, walking toward a one room school house.

I told her I liked the drawing.

"Well, that picture reminds me of walking to school with my sisters," she said.

Back in the car, we headed further into the woods that surrounded the restaurant, out to the state park. My father picked up his driving monologue, Jesus this and Jesus that. And I caught salient phrases: "Christianity is a step higher than Judaism." "Medical records of virgin birth."

"Could I ask you a favor?" Dwayne piped up. "You know we're Jewish, and Jesus is not part of our religion. Would you mind talking about something else?"

"Oh, of course. Of course." A long silence followed until my father began, "You Know Who once said."

But somewhere among references to You Know Who, my father switched to Moses. "The greatest man in the Old Testament," he pronounced. "God used Moses to do important things, even though Moses killed a man."

Clearly he viewed Moses' slaying of the man who was beating a slave as an act that God would not have condoned.

"God used Moses to do important things, even though Moses killed a man," seemed to be a statement he clung to. He'd written similar words to me in one of his first letters.

From Moses, my father turned to a subject that seemed for a moment to be entirely unrelated. "You were a much wanted baby, Ingrid. Your mother and I wanted you.

"I would still be married to her, but I did something I shouldn't have."

Right there with Dottie in the front seat of the car beside him, he said that as if he still regretted the divorce.

Maybe this was intended as a confession that his behavior had caused the divorce. He, like Moses, had done something terrible. So reprehensible it had ended his precious marriage and happy family.

The blow that had ended their marriage.

"I did something I shouldn't have."

Did I have the answer for what had sent him into what I thought of as "religious therapy"?

I thought of the day he'd reined himself in after he threw me over his shoulder outside my high school to carry me into the principal's office and declare himself my father. When I yelled and begged, he'd put me down and driven me home, never to mention the subject again.

WE ENTERED THE TRAIL over a flat wooden bridge above a stream. Two walls of evergreens and bare branched trees leaned over the stream as far in the distance as I could see. I stopped to look down at the froth where the water skipped over a ridge of rocks. My father stood beside me.

"Hiking is my only sport," I told him. "I hated P.E. in school. I'm not very coordinated."

"Have you ever lost your footing and caught your balance?"

"Yes."

"Then you're not uncoordinated."

I looked up at him.

My father and I stepped onto the red dirt trail and entered the woods. Up ahead, Dwayne was saying to Dottie, "Ingrid and I backpacked in Arizona and Utah."

WE DROVE OUT of the state park into more farmland until my father stated, "Our little town," as we passed a gas station and convenience store and headed into fields again.

White wood with narrow green shutters, their one story house stretched between a tall, thick trunked tree on one side to a dainty evergreen on the other. I saw a mountain range in the distance and felt a hollow loneliness out there on that road far away from any other house.

We parked beside a white picket fence and entered the house through the kitchen.

"Let's all rest now and meet in the kitchen for dinner at six," my father said. "I'll show you around after dinner."

He led us down a hall past their bedroom into what he called "our guest room." A high queen bed and dark wood dresser filled the room. An oval rag rug lay on the wood floor. I hoisted myself onto the bed to sit beside Dwayne and read in the hour we had before dinner.

MY FATHER AND DOTTIE had dressed for dinner. He, in a maroon dress shirt with tiny white polka dots and navy wool pants with a thin maroon plaid. She, in a shiny blue blouse hanging loose over gray wool pants. We'd remained in the jeans, pullovers, and sneakers we'd arrived in.

A laminated flower print cloth lay on a table at the crook in the L-shaped space where the kitchen became the living room. The table's placement, perpendicular to the kitchen cabinets, allowed Dottie access to the stove, sink, and counter, with my father seated beside her. He motioned for us to sit on the living room side.

I placed a foil wrapped cake on the table. "I made my favorite apple cake for you. My cousins call it 'Ingrid's cake.' I carried it in my backpack, so it wouldn't get smashed in the suitcase."

"Why thank you, Ingrid." My father picked up the package. "We will certainly enjoy this."

Dottie set a serving plate of green beans and small boiled potatoes before us. "You all go ahead and serve yourselves," she invited.

She placed a platter of greasy steak in front of my father, and as he carved it into pieces, Dottie apologized that they "couldn't find one more marbled."

He resumed his religious monologue until we finished the vanilla ice cream. During dessert, I interjected quietly—to make clear I was not intending to argue—that I respected his religion and valued moral behavior but didn't believe in a God who speaks to every person.

"Good," he said. "Honesty is the first step."

Dottie reached for our empty ice cream bowls and shooed away my hand as she had over the empty dinner plates. My father rose. "I promised to show you around. First, I'll show you where I work."

We followed him into their bedroom past tightly tucked twin beds to the far wall where a guitar case leaned against a desk. I saw an unframed baby picture of me on the desk.

"This is where I write my compositions.

"And that's a bust I made of you, Ingrid." He pointed to a red clay bust of a girl with a pony tail on a nearby shelf.

"Now, the living room."

He led us back down the hall to an upright piano where *Hymns for the Family of God*, sheet music for *Sweet Little Jesus Boy*, and sheet music by Stephen Foster leaned side by side on the piano rack. On a long table beside the piano, a porcelain plate with the face of Queen Elizabeth stood beside a white ceramic box with a tiny blue bird handle and a three inch tall ceramic boy.

I knew Aunt Kanka made the box and the boy. I had her ceramics, too.

At the far end of this table, stood a wooden chair for a small child, the back and legs painted green and decorated with white flowers.

"I wrote you that your little chair from my house in Alexandria is in our living room."

He'd lived in that house while I lived with Tante Sonja, Uncle Rob, Moms, and Lenny. He'd sent the picture of me sitting in that chair, but I didn't remember that house. I didn't tell him.

Next on our living room tour, an oil painting of a red brick house among tall palm trees. A path wound from the front door to a sign in the grass which read *Tyler's Haven of Harmony*, printed above a treble clef.

"This was our house in Florida, before my allergies became so bad we moved up here."

Dottie had joined us from the kitchen. "My sister, Jewel, lives here in North Carolina. I'm a Tar Heel."

"No-o-o-w," my father enunciated, "we would like to si-i-i-ng for you. Please take a seat." He motioned to the three or four straight backed wooden chairs in the room.

While Dwayne and I positioned our chairs, my father brought in his guitar and sat on the piano bench facing us. Dottie stood beside him. He blew through a tuner, strummed a few strings, tightened them, and plucked one.

"Hm-m-m-m. Hm-m-m-m." They both found the note and began to sing. The song was about two "sweethearts" pledging their faithfulness. They followed with a nonsense song about a frog that said "Ree deep." My father introduced the next song. "A friend in the Back to God Movement asked me to write a song about the importance of prayer in the schools. This song came to me while I was fishing."

It was a song about the students, faculty, and principal of a public school who all prayed together for a boy's sick mother even though prayer in public school is forbidden. And it was clearly a Christian prayer. I sat on that hard backed chair—like the girl to whom they'd sung about a manger in their hearts in the motel room years before— and I wondered if it would have made any difference to him if I'd talked to him during my childhood, if I'd told him how oppressed I felt being subjected to Christian prayers in school, and if I'd explained my reason for those feelings. He and Dottie seemed like such kind people. Would they empathize? Would he have written this song?

WHEN WE ARRIVED at the table for breakfast, Dottie had American cheese omelets ready to slip onto our plates. My father confirmed that we wanted toast and popped bread into the toaster.

"We bought you whole wheat bread," he said.

This referred to our telephone conversation about the plans for our trip. They'd asked what we eat for breakfast.

"I'm not sure I did the right thing though," Dottie confessed. She stuck a fork into a saucepan on the stove and pulled out some cooked spinach. "When you said you eat omelets with cheese and spinach, is this what you meant?"

"Actually," I began, "we cook raw spinach inside our omelets, but…"

"But we'll enjoy the cooked spinach with our omelets." Dwayne finished my sentence.

Spinach still dangling off the fork in her hand, Dottie stood at the stove and laughed. "I thought I got that wrong."

Watching her laugh at herself so easily, I felt closer to her.

When she joined us at the table, Dottie spooned some molasses out of a jar and ate it. "For my bones." She smiled and began to tell us about herself. We learned she had two older sisters. They all grew up in Clemmons, near Winston-Salem, in a house in the woods. "Our town was so small, my sisters and I could walk all over it by ourselves.

"This town here, isn't much bigger. Makes me feel at home."

"We have a gift for you," my father announced as Dottie cleared the table.

He gave us their record with the songs they'd sung the night before and many others.

"We also want to buy you a copy of the Bible," he added. "We'll send it to you."

One hour and many "You Know Who's" later, we were on the tarmac beside the airplane, hugging and promising to write and call.

DWAYNE AND I SAT side by side at our dining room table, leftover Kung Pao chicken on our plates, the carved wooden chopsticks Dwayne had brought from China, waiting on our napkins. Dwayne opened a bottle of red wine and poured for each of us. We sipped and began to blurt out impressions.

"They're depressing," I started.

"Like their town," Dwayne added.

"They catered to us."

"With the food."

"And the walk."

Dwayne poured more wine and smiled, "His invention! His puns!"

"We may share a love of nature, but he's not *fun* for me." I took a huge gulp of wine. "That would be OK if he weren't my father."

We traded more impressions.

I finished what was left in my glass and looked at Dwayne. "Did we unleash the possibility that he can claim a part in our life?"

"It's alright to draw lines. We can let him in the way we want." Dwayne picked up the bottle and shook the last drops into my glass. "We finished it!" he laughed. A bottle that usually would have lasted us three days.

"It's culture shock," I concluded.

"AUNT LIPPY, WE'RE BACK, and I couldn't wait to call you."

"Oh, Ingrid, how was it?"

"Well, they were very nice to us."

I described the weekend.

"But, Aunt Lippy, he never stops talking about his religion."

"His religion depresses me, Ingrid. Do you know what he did to me and Bill when we visited them? He wouldn't let us sleep in their house because we're not married!"

26

THE CLEAREST PICTURE I HAVE OF MY FATHER WHEN HE WAS married to my mother comes from Tante Sonja. I told her Dwayne and I had visited him in North Carolina. She said, "Your father's a good man, such a good man." And she told me two stories.

Frans Hernandez, one of Tante Sonja and Uncle Rob's Dutch friends, was at their apartment for dinner along with my mother and father. After dinner, Frans did a magic trick with his tie and a scissors that made it look as if he'd cut the tie into two pieces. When he let go, the tie was still in one piece. My father wanted to try the trick. Frans warned him not to.

"He had plenty of warnings," Tante Sonja said, "but he said he could do it."

My father cut his tie.

"He cried when he cut it," she said. "A grown man crying about cutting his tie. For years, every time we saw Frans, we talked about Bay Tay crying."

No matter how many times Tante Sonja repeated, "He was a good man, such a good man," nothing could mask what this story revealed.

The second story was about the time my father saw Moms pushing me in a baby carriage outside Woodworth & Lothrop in Washington, D.C.

"He tried to grab you, but Moms screamed for the police and held onto you."

When Tante Sonja told me this story, it was early in my marriage. I rooted for Moms, glad she'd won the struggle. I still am. But when I became a parent, I could imagine my father's desperation upon encountering his child, the child who had been carried away from his apartment while he was at work.

Maybe he was on his lunch break, walking down the sidewalk near his office. A few weeks earlier he'd lost his whole life in one day. It was all he could think about when he didn't force himself to keep his mind on work. One night, he and Sienie had argued. She'd gone to get a towel from the linen closet to give Ingrid a bath. The scene was engraved on his mind. Sienie stood there facing him, a towel in one hand, the other hand pressing Ingrid to her shoulder.

"You treat me like a child," she'd said. "Giving me an allowance, not telling me how much money we have!"

That's how his parents had done things. Couldn't she understand that was how things should be? He was taking care of her.

"Now, Sweetheart," he'd said. "I don't want to worry you with those things. You've got enough to do with taking care of Ingrid and shopping and cooking—and cleaning."

"Ya!" she spat at him. "I'm a servant! That's how you see me."

He couldn't understand why she was upset. His mother had always seemed so happy doing these things. His father had gone off to work every day and taken care of all their money matters, too. He remembered seeing Daddy hand Mother her household money at the end of the week. Mother had stood there, her blond hair pulled back into a loose knot at the nape of her neck, her blue eyes solemn for a moment before she had smiled and offered a quiet, "Thank you, Edgar."

Sienie tossed her dark hair back with a shake of her head and carried Ingrid over to the bathtub. "In my home," she said, depositing Ingrid into the water, "my mother ran a shoe store. She didn't sit at home cleaning. She and my father both handled their financial affairs."

He didn't know what to say. He felt so unsure of himself. Why did she have to turn things upside down when he had their life arranged the way it should be? "In my home," he shouted, "you'll do things my way!"

"I won't," she said in a steady voice, "if it means being paid every week as if I were your servant."

He knew he shouldn't do it even while it was happening. For a moment he saw the image of his mother accepting the money with her docile grace. Then rage took over, and he was striking that insolent black haired woman full and hard in the face with the palm of his hand.

She received the blow with a stunning strength. She didn't stagger backward or fall but seemed to turn in one movement away from the impact of his hand toward the bath. She stooped, swept up the child into the towel, and pushed past him to run into the bedroom. He followed, but the bedroom door swung shut, and the lock clicked.

"Sweetheart!" he shouted. "Sweetheart!" There was no reply. He staggered to the couch and wept. He thought he heard Ingrid's voice and Sienie shushing her. He might have heard Sienie singing softly to the child. But afterwards there was only silence. He wept into that silence. Long into the night he wept, until he slumped into sleep on the couch.

He'd gone to work the next morning, and while he was away, his Sienie had left the apartment carrying Ingrid with her.

So many nights he'd lain awake thinking of Ingrid. Her tiny pearly fingers limp on the sheet while she slept. Ingrid leaning back against his legs when she was tired. Ingrid grinning with delight when he pretended to take a coin from her ear. Ingrid throwing her arms around his neck as he hoisted her up when he came home from work every evening. How could Sienie steal her away! He'd ached at his inability to be near his child. The ache still kept him awake at night and followed him in the daytime.

Now, as he turned the corner at the entrance to Woodworth & Lothrop, there was Sienie's mother right in front of him, with little Ingrid in a baby carriage. He ran toward her. He grabbed her. She looked at him, and her face lit in a smile. The smile changed into shocked fear. But he had no chance to soothe her. Sienie's mother was hitting him with her pocketbook and screaming, "Police! Police!"

"You devil!" he yelled. "She's my child. My little girl. She's mine!" he wailed. But Sienie's mother hit him hard in the jaw with the corner of her black leather pocketbook. He let go his grasp on Ingrid's arms, Sienie's mother still slamming him in the head with one hand, her other holding fast to Ingrid's shoulder.

He backed away. "Don't worry, Honeybunch," he called to Ingrid as Sienie's mother pushed the carriage, "I'll see you. I'll see you real soon, Honeybunch."

27

HE WROTE FIRST, A CARD THANKING US FOR OUR VISIT.

Life has more meaning now, he quoted himself saying to Dottie as they drove home from the airport.

Yes, it's fuller. More complete, he quoted her replying.

And thanking us for *"Ingrid's cake," specially backpacked in, and which gets better day by day.*

The trip resolved the confusion that had catapulted me back and forth between the two worlds in my life since the arrival of the letter from the lawyer in Crawfordsville two years earlier. In the few weeks before I wrote to thank them, I settled into myself. I saw my father through my eyes. The threat of my own Shvantzness and crazy streak slid away.

It was easy now to address him as "Dad," and I knew what I wanted to say.

I thanked them for everything, and continued,

Now I see you both as the warm and kind people that you are, not as the ogres I'd been led to imagine. Now I better understand the behavior of all the adults involved in my custody and related matters. I recognize that these adults all made mistakes. I also understand, without anger, why decisions were made and actions were taken on all sides.

I feel just as sorry for my parents who deserved to start their marriage, and our family, with a clean slate, as I do for you who wanted to share a life with his daughter, including correspondence and recognition as her father. I've asked myself repeatedly how to handle the custody and upbringing of a child whose parents live extremely different lives, without completely confusing the child. Certainly there were problems for me in the way my custody and upbringing were handled, but I can say that I suffered far less from our family's divorce than have many children in a divorce.

What pulled at me most was my father's comment about what ended his marriage to my mother. I would never condone his impulsive violence, but he already blamed himself sufficiently for that. I couldn't let him continue to blame himself alone for the marriage ending.

Dad, you said that had you not done some foolish—or wrong—thing, you and my mother would likely still be married. I want to emphasize my certainty it was not your action that caused the divorce. My mother made a mistake.

She had fled a rich, happy existence to save her life. She lived in terror. She has nightmares all these years later. She escaped death innumerable times, and even when she reached haven in Surinam, was almost taken into a German U-boat.

When she met you, she was afraid to be Jewish. It probably even seemed stupid and unnecessary to her to be Jewish. She tried to change herself, not only into a Christian, but also into the proper wife for you. But she found that she could not—out of love for a kind man and with an intellectual determination to be different—change her own character. When she learned this, she probably felt the self-hatred that results from making such a serious mistake. She no doubt felt terribly sorry for dragging a decent man and a baby into this predicament, too. My mother obviously loved you, Dad, when she married you. She obviously believed she could turn herself into a religious Christian as well as into an appropriate wife for you. My mother does not act without conviction.

You must understand that she was, and is, extremely different from you.

I described her growing up in the main business district of The Hague, her education, and her Jewish life.

Jewish traditions were so heavily woven into her life that she could never entirely extricate her emotions from them. She would detest isolation from others and must live in a place where she can meet other Europeans. She accepts nothing on faith, believing only what appeals to her logic.

I addressed the issue he had made paramount:

> *Judaism is against actively converting people, and I agree with this position. Our people have been the victims of intolerance for so long that we would not force our views on others.*

> *You've been part of the majority in this country—Christian—so you don't know what it's like to stand in class and pray to someone else's vision of God. I know. I had to do it all through grade school. I do not understand proselytizing. If a person values a particular religion, fine. But why force others to?*

He answered:

> *Please believe that these are my basic feelings: I want you to have the best things in your life, <u>as you determine them</u> to be the best.*

> *I will say now that your visit was a great highlight of my life.*

My father never gave us the Bible.

28

WE DREW LINES. MY FATHER DID, TOO.

He understood my unwillingness to bring my two families together. *Ingrid dear,* he wrote, *thank you for being honest about your feelings when I asked for Sonja and Rob's address. Of course we don't have to write them. I have found that my own emotional capacity was not prepared for that move.*

He made it clear they wouldn't stay with us after we moved into a house. He had told us in North Carolina they'd made intermittent visits to the Washington area since leaving years earlier and had always stayed at a campground because they needed to spread out. They would continue this practice, he wrote, when they visited us. Dwayne and I were grateful for this suggestion, which would allow all of us to retreat to our own environments overnight and reflect on the day we spent together. My father recognized we each needed to integrate our lives at our own emotional pace.

They were in no rush to visit. Six months after our visit, my father explained that their music projects came first.

We're deeply involved in creating a four-part music arrangement and in efforts to line up capable singers and a good brass group to help with our second recording.

Also we hope to be in touch soon with a company in Kentucky that may be interested in our work. It's even possible we might have to make a trip there.

Please hold a good thought for our strength.

He was sixty-nine with few wrinkles and a healthy gait when he'd walked with us through the state park in North Carolina.

WE WORKED, (I studied tax law, too), found a house, and moved in. A year and a half after we visited them, my father and Dottie drove to a camp ground near D.C. for one weekend, to meet our six-month-old son.

"I want him to call me Granddaddy." My father looked down at his only grandson who, installed on my father's lap, smiled at Dwayne.

We sat at our round Danish modern kitchen table where we'd served my father and Dottie our omelets filled with spinach and Jarlsberg cheese, whole grain toast, fruit, and French roast coffee. Nearby, stood the presents my father had brought for his grandson, the small wooden chair we'd seen in their living room—the chair my father said I sat in when I lived with Tante Sonja and Uncle Rob and visited my father on the weekends—and the wooden sled he'd used as a young boy in Crawfordsville.

TWO MONTHS LATER, the phone rang one evening. Dwayne answered and passed it to me with a puzzled look. "The caller says he's your brother."

"Ingrid, it's George, your brother."

"Oh." *My brother, he calls himself!* "Hello."

"I'm calling to tell you our father is dead."

Our father?! "What happened?" I spoke quietly.

"My mother drove him out to his communing spot and waited for him. He had a heart attack and died before he made it back to the car."

George told me the funeral arrangements. I said I couldn't make it.

I couldn't stand before his congregation to receive their condolences as his daughter. I wasn't ready to make a public declaration to anyone of my relationship to my father. I was still groping through my feelings. To recognize my love for him. To explain to myself how this love affected my identity. To somehow bring the two worlds together inside myself.

And I couldn't stand beside George as his sister. We'd seen each other a few times two decades earlier in the world that didn't exist where I'd hidden myself from him. I couldn't pretend now that we had a relationship we'd never had—anywhere.

I sent flowers to Dottie. I phoned her after the funeral. For the rest of her life, we exchanged letters and cards.

My father was seventy years old.

"YOU'RE LUCKY," Dad stated in our weekly phone call. "He did you a favor."

I thought he was wrong. I believed that with the lines my father and I had both drawn, my life could have contained my father and Dottie along with my parents. I hadn't told my parents how little my father encroached. I hadn't troubled them with the details of our trip to North Carolina, of the letters, of the phone calls. I thought telling my parents all of that would have hurt them. I knew Dad remembered how my father resented his exclusion from most of my life and how I'd returned from my afternoons with him to report the ways he'd made me miserable, like when he read to me from the New Testament and threw me over his shoulder to take me into my school. I knew Dad wanted to protect me. I thought he was wrong, but I said nothing.

Now I could comprehend the religious wording in my father's first letter to me.

> *Your loving gesture of writing to me can change our lives, like being upheld by the hand of the Lord through his divine touch, if we are aware of the opportunity to offer, each to the other, the best of our understanding, love, and compassion. I'll pray to be helped to do this, on my part.*

My father and I had achieved the goal he'd set for us.

My father had taught me the power of reaching out to another person—the power of touch. I wished I could tell him.

Part Two

1

I STILL HELD MY MOTHER'S SECRET INSIDE ME, A SOLEMN obligation. And, as always, I divulged little of my life to others.

Secrecy was my hidden career.

While other mothers at our kids' elementary school formed friendships, I occasionally met someone for a cup of tea at her kitchen table or mine, while the kids played. But I managed to avoid the kind of friendships in which women discuss their lives way back to childhood.

Marguerite placed the porcelain tea pot on her kitchen table and tossed her straight black hair out of her face. We'd met a week earlier at Back to School Night where we established we'd each been named by a European mother and that our sons were friends. She poured the tea into porcelain tea cups just like my mother did. The boys were in the family room with a pile of Legos.

Marguerite picked up one of the sugar cookies I'd brought, dunked it in her tea, and bit off a piece. "Tell me about your work," she prompted.

I summarized my tax law job in a few sentences, mentioned that I was lucky to work part time, and asked about her job.

"Oh, I worked as a real estate attorney. I was glad to quit when Chris was born. I'd had enough."

I asked question after question about her former work, where she grew up, her mother's European background, what it was like for Marguerite to grow up part European, and whether she liked to read. We discovered we liked many of the same authors, and I centered the rest of the conversation on books.

"Maybe we can meet more often for tea while the boys play," she suggested.

"I can't plan anything regular," I said. "I rarely have time for a relaxing afternoon like this. I'm either working or grocery shopping and cooking. This was really fun." I assured her the college student who picked up my son from school was completely reliable. She could drive both boys to our house to play after school. My hedge to avoid telling her about myself.

On the occasional afternoons I was able to pick up our son from school, I saw other mothers in front of me on the sidewalk hugging each other and chattering.

INSTALLED IN FRONT of my computer screen, I scrutinized a Tax Court case and highlighted pertinent paragraphs as I scrolled through the document. I heard my office mates talking and laughing across the space between their cubicles. Tension pounded in my chest. Only two more hours before I had to switch into sneakers and sprint to the subway. Only two more hours to finish the first draft of the document I was writing.

Two other lawyers from our branch burst through the door beside my desk. "Come on," they yelled at my office mates. "We're about to miss our lunch reservation!"

Only a quick "hello" in my direction. I'd built a reputation. I raced to my desk every morning, switched from sneakers to heels, made tea while my computer started, and—entrenched at my desk—read case files, researched online, drafted documents, ate my peanut butter sandwich and banana—and avoided conversation, so I could work part time and run home early to be with the kids while they did their homework at that round Danish modern kitchen table.

SINCE LAW SCHOOL, we'd met with Dwight's longtime friends on the weekends. With them, too, I dwelt on books, politics, and as little below the surface of my life as possible.

Until loneliness triggered a change.

Dwayne had to cancel a two-week trip we'd planned to the Canadian Rockies. A year earlier, he'd had a hip replacement at an unusually young age. His year old hip had begun to hurt so much he was limping. He would substitute physical therapy for hiking. To meet the hotel cancellation deadlines, Dwayne called hotels from our daughter's camp the day we arrived to take her home. I trudged through the dusty heat with our daughter to see the four girl tent where she'd lived all summer.

Dwayne stowed the camp duffel in the trunk. I settled behind the steering wheel and bumped the car over the dirt parking lot, out of the camp. I was headed back to our D.C. suburb and two weeks of unexpected commuting to work instead of hiking in the Canadian Rockies. I merged the car onto the highway and began to sob, "I don't want to go back to my life. I don't want to go back to my life."

"Mommy, pull onto the shoulder and let Daddy drive!"

"No! I can do it!"

I faced the highway through a blur of tears that entire forty-five minute drive.

And spent the two vacation weeks at home.

Early each morning, I strode over the dirt path through the woods behind our neighborhood. Beside the creek, past the mossy rocks, up the hill to our street, I followed my thoughts.

Mom deserves to keep her secret. We all deserve to decide what our lives look like. But how is this affecting me? My life is part of her secret! I really don't want to tell everyone my story. I like being Sienie and Benny's daughter with the Jewish image they bestowed on me. That image is what I am—not a façade. To explain what I want people to understand about my double worlds would be too much trouble. OK. I can continue to offer the abridged version of my life. But I'm keeping too much secret. I'm trapped in here! Something's got to come out.

I unlocked the front door, ran into the kitchen, drank a mug of tea, ate a bowl of cereal, and scribbled on a legal pad. With a second mug of tea, I ran downstairs to my computer to craft my thoughts into poems and stories.

"YOU DON'T NEED to keep everything in your life secret."

Dwayne looked at me over his wine glass. We'd let the kids go inside, down to the basement playroom, while we finished dinner. Dwayne and I stayed on the deck and watched the green of the surrounding trees deepen as the sun began to set. I'd spilled out my thoughts about the ingrained secrecy.

"We all pick and choose what we tell—and who we tell it to," he continued.

I wadded up my napkin and put it on my empty plate.

"You have to trust someone—sometime. You can even talk about your father if you want to. Just don't tell her friends. You won't ruin her life. But with all that silence, you might ruin yours."

The woods were dark. Together we picked up the dishes and placemats and carried them into the kitchen.

I put the dishes on the counter, turned to Dwayne, hugged him, and held on. We could hear the kids laughing in the basement.

AFTER THOSE TWO WEEKS of contemplation, I talked to more people, at work and elsewhere, and revealed an aspect or two of my life as I encountered people who shared them. Colleagues at work tried to pry me away from my solitary routine—and I let them.

"You have a wicked sense of humor," my new office mate said. "I've never had such good laughs."

Every morning I regaled him with vignettes from my metro commutes into D.C. "Let's schedule five minute chat-and-laugh breaks every two hours," my office mate suggested. "You can limit them with that alarm on your watch."

A colleague shared stories about her grandmother who was so much like Moms that we forged a friendship. Every few weeks, one of us would call the other and ask, "Can you eat lunch in my office today?"

I allowed myself to fit a few minutes of personal conversation in with the legal issues whenever I consulted about a case with someone. I stood in the hall briefly and chatted instead of running past. Soon people knocked on my door, stuck their heads in, and asked to sit and talk.

And at home, I spent hours at my kitchen table with Linda— while our sons played. We sought each other's advice about our children, discussed books, travel, and frustrations with our mothers, and helped each other with the kids' birthday parties. Our son had found a best friend, and I had found his mother.

2

IN ADDITION TO TANTE SONJA, I TOLD TANTE NANNIE AND UNCLE
Hal we'd met my father. They echoed Tante Sonja, reassuring me
he was a good man. Tante Nannie said she exchanged New Year's
cards with Aunt Lippy every January and had done the same with
Aunt Kanka and Aunt Mary Frances during their lives. "His
sisters were wonderful people."

Uncle Hal recounted a memory. "Your biological father drove
over to show me his new Buick. It had portholes in the fender for
the air to go through to cool the engine. He was very proud of that
Buick."

Uncle Hal remembered the Buick Pecial!

I'd told my parent substitutes and received their reassurances,
but I wasn't ready to discuss my father with my cousins or my
brother.

I did want to talk with Marcie. I'd never had a closer friend since we met in religious school in first grade, when our families had also become close.

"I've forgotten what it's like to take care of a baby." The tiny head fit in the palm of my hand as I balanced it and scooped the little body from the blanket on the living room carpet into my arms.

Marcie had flown up from Texas to care for her newborn twin grandchildren in her daughter and son-in-law's Virginia townhouse. I'd made the hour drive from our home, between hills of snow the plows had thrown onto the shoulders of the beltway. Since we'd graduated from college, we'd only seen each other twice and communicated a few times.

We fed the babies and put them down on the blankets in the living room while we sat beside them to eat our turkey sandwiches and avocado salads. All morning, while we prepared food, fed the babies, and now while we ate, we relived our post-college years, explaining to each other—and to ourselves—the decisions we'd made since then. Throughout, videos ran in my mind of Marcie and me kicking our legs in the air in my apartment or in her living room as we made up dances to the musicals on my parents' records or to Frank Sinatra.

"Marcie, there's something I have to tell you."

The babies were asleep on the blankets. Marcie and I sat near them on two straight backed dining room chairs and faced each other over mugs of hot tea.

"I've been keeping a secret from you the whole time I've known you. Dad is not my birth father."

My tea mug cradled in my lap and forgotten, in a few sentences I gave the woman I'd called my sister since age six the bare facts about my father and his visits. And I told her Mom had pledged me to secrecy. "To me Dad is my real father," I ended.

Marcie looked at me. "I've known this for a long time. Mother told me and Frank when I was in junior high school. She said not to tell anybody and not to talk to you about it."

"You knew! But how? Did my mother tell your parents?!"

She couldn't have done that. I knew she couldn't have.

"No. When you first moved to Houston, you told the Kleinmanns you had two daddies. They told my parents."

I stared at Marcie and thought, *That was the Ingrid who told her visiting daddy she'd always be thinking of him—before he became The Shvantz.*

"Marcie, do you know what a difference it would have made if I'd discussed this with you and your parents? It's not your fault—or theirs. You had to pretend you didn't know. My father came to visit me every Christmas vacation and every summer while you were at camp. I could never tell you what I'd been doing. I had a secret life—even from you. I promised my mother."

I told her my mother called my father The Shvantz, how that made me feel, how the secrecy had spread and left me lonely.

Marcie and I had grown up in each other's homes. Her parents were like my own. Her father had taught about The Holocaust and had supported my decision to teach about it. They knew my mother, the details of her escape, and understood how she was affected. If only I could have poured out my self-doubts and confusion to Marcie's parents and asked for advice during their lives, my life could have been much easier.

Of course, I'd never done that with my aunts and uncles, though they knew The Secret. My pledge to my mother had closed me into myself.

As I told Marcie now, another layer of shame dropped away.

3

"INKY, THERE'S SOMETHING I WANT TO TELL YOU."

This seemed like a mild statement in the middle of what had recently become a regular Sunday morning phone call from my brother. Neill, now in his early twenties, married, with a one year old son, was mad at Mom and Dad and trying to figure things out by talking to me.

Neill continued, "When I was fourteen, I spent a week with Tante Sonja and Uncle Rob in the summer, the way I always did after camp ended.

"Well, one morning when I was alone with Tante Sonja at breakfast, she referred to 'Ingrid's father' right in the middle of our conversation."

The subject we'd never discussed.

"Inky, I acted like I knew what she was talking about."

That day, Neill told me, instead of going to the Library of Congress to do research for his debate team while Tante Sonja and

Uncle Rob were at work, Neill went to the D.C. Court House and found Mom's marriage certificate to Bill Tyler. At the end of the week, he took the train up to Connecticut to stay with Tante Nannie, Uncle Hal, and our three cousins. Neill dropped "Ingrid's father" into conversations with each cousin and confirmed that they all knew about Bill Tyler.

"Everyone in the family knew about your father—except me! Why didn't Mom and Dad trust me enough to tell me?"

"Neill, they trust you. Mom was probably afraid you'd look down on her for being a divorcee. She's so afraid of what people will think, she made me keep it a secret."

I gave him the facts: the divorce, my vow of secrecy, and the fact that my father visited. I omitted the details and emotions.

And I said what I'd been thinking for years—that I assumed he didn't know, because he'd never said anything. That I didn't tell him because I was afraid he'd look down on me for having come from an inferior father.

"Inky, I would never feel that way about you. And I understand why you didn't say anything. It was Mom and Dad's job to tell me. They're big liars."

I told him about Mom's five miscarriages. That she'd once said, "A woman wants to have a child from the man she loves." I told him how much Neill meant to Mom and Dad. They'd wanted him for over a decade.

But while I said all of that, I thought about the shock he'd had when his understanding of his whole family changed—and I savored my immense relief that he accepted me. Neill's birth had been the most important event in my life when I was fourteen. He was the boy who lined up his miniature cars and trucks, who called me "Wee Wee" on my high school campus, who gave me the chance to take him on adventures to ice cream shops and the office of a famous magazine. I'd watched him grow into his high school's top debater and their newspaper editor. His incisive mind had taken him to a leading university and helped him make sound decisions as an adult. That brother of mine had whooped when the law school president handed me my diploma. I couldn't bear to lose his respect.

Mom and Dad needed to know what Neill had been holding in for ten years. They could talk to him and bring him back to them—to our family. I called them immediately. Mom answered.

"Mom, Neill just called. He told me something that's going to be hard for you to hear." I repeated the conversation. I included the reason I'd never discussed my father with him.

"That's so mean!" Mom exploded. "Sonja knew I hadn't told him. When he was born I made her promise never to say anything to Neill until I told him. Don't you think that was mean of Tante Sonja?"

"Mom, how was she supposed to know whether you told him or not? Neill was fourteen years old! Can you imagine how he felt? How he still feels? His whole world turned upside down. When were you planning to tell him?"

"Sonja's jealous of me, and she's trying to hurt me."

"Mom, I think you and Dad should talk to Neill about the divorce and explain why you kept it secret. Tell him how much you trust, love, and respect him."

"Yah, Ingrid, thank you!" Mom answered in her coldest tone.

4

MOM WAS THE PERSON WITH WHOM I MOST WANTED TO DISCUSS my two worlds.

When I'd come home from elementary school, she'd asked me about my day. I knew she wanted to hear everything I'd done and seen and thought about. I knew she was my best friend and cared about me more than anyone else did—except Dad. I could tell her all my problems and ask for advice—all my problems except my biggest one—the problem she'd made.

From the day she'd called my father The Shvantz, I'd sensed that the most I could tell Mom or Dad was my great discomfort with my father's inscriptions in the books he sent, or something negative about my father or Dottie. I couldn't say: When I walk out to his car, I have to change my behavior. If I'm nice to him, I'll betray you, because you're calling him The Shvantz. I couldn't ask my mother, Why is it OK for me to wheedle expensive gifts out of him when I'm never allowed to ask you for anything? Does Neill know about my father? Because I'm afraid to tell Neill. I'm afraid he'll look down on me because I come from a Shvantz, when Neill's father is a surgeon. I was afraid to say that I felt inferior to my cousins, too, because they had real fathers they could be proud of. And maybe I was crazy because my father was.

And from the day Mom had turned my father's existence into a secret, I sensed she and Dad didn't want to face it themselves. They'd already taught me you could inoculate a book by replacing the inscription and make part of reality disappear. The Secret had turned a significant part of my life into the world that didn't exist. How could I discuss that world with the mother who had created it—unless she brought it up, like when she said my aunts were good people? Mom had confirmed in that phone conversation after I'd written about my decision to meet my father—the first time I'd asked Mom to discuss the world that didn't exist—that she wished to talk about it as little as possible.

I wanted to be able to discuss my father, my aunts, my grandparents—and all the facts I'd learned about that family—on the telephone with Mom or inside the walls of her house or Dwayne's and my house—even one time.

I wanted to pull the me who had only lived in the world that did not exist into the real world—along with the rest of me. My whole adult life I wanted the catharsis she had from her interview at the Holocaust Museum. She told me that talking about her escape had made her feel better than she'd felt for years.

"By talking about it, it becomes less frightening," she'd said. "It just becomes part of life."

I wanted my life to feel more normal, more accepted, not something shameful that had to be hidden. I knew what could do that for me: to discuss with my mother all of my feelings and experiences in the passages between my two worlds.

Or maybe I just wanted to feel closer to her, like we really were best friends.

My mother had done something shocking at the end of her interview at the Holocaust Museum. After they stopped recording, she continued to look at the psychiatrist who had conducted the interview.

"I married a non-Jew soon after I arrived in Washington, D.C.," she stated. "He was my daughter's father."

Stunned, I sat alone upstairs behind the glass wall and stared down at my mother. I'd never heard her mention the marriage to anyone.

The psychiatrist said nothing.

On the subway back to Maryland, my mother thanked me for convincing her to give the interview. It had taken months of persuasion.

"The story of your escape is important," I'd repeated in innumerable phone calls. "You only talk about it to Holocaust survivors.

"Mom," I insisted, "other people need to know your story."

She had finally listened.

In the subway parking lot, as my mother and I walked between the rows of cars, as casually as if she were asking whether we needed to drive far to reach the deli where we planned to have lunch, my mother said, "There's only one thing in my life I'm ashamed of—my first marriage."

I proceeded through that sea of cars, focused only on what had just been thrust at me. She still felt shame after all those years. Shame about her first marriage—more than mere embarrassment at being a divorcee. Dad hadn't talked away this shame the way he talked away my problems. Dad's complete acceptance of her and her little daughter and the open arms of Grandma, Grandpa, Aunt Julia, and Uncle Joe hadn't squelched it.

The day my mother was able to make this revelation, I was unable to respond. I needed to think.

We reached my car, and I drove her to our favorite deli where a small barrel of pickles sat on the table between us. We ate corned beef sandwiches and pickles while my mother expounded on the release she felt after recounting the story of her escape at the Holocaust Museum that morning.

My mother's shame was tangled up with everything else I hoped to discuss with her now, years after her interview. I wanted to eradicate that shame, and I knew what to say.

I decided to start with a letter.

Dear Mom,

All through my life, I've had to go somewhere alone and cry whenever I've come close to feeling the emotions I buried about your flight from the Netherlands and the effects of the Holocaust on you.

So, yesterday, after I drove you over to Tante Sonja's, after hearing you talk to Rachel's class about your escape, I sobbed for all the grief you've felt—still feel.

Just as your life stories are important to you, so are mine to me. And so is my identity. Yes, you and Dad are my parents. I've never questioned that, and I'm proud you're my parents. But I want to know as much as possible about all three of my families—yours, Dad's, and my father's. I can't pretend part of me doesn't exist. It exists, and it excites me.

Aunt Lippy gave me a written family history and family tree. It's hilarious and fascinating to me that some of my ancestors fought in the Revolutionary War—me, whose family fled the Holocaust and pogroms! I'm pleased to have a great cousin who went to Williams and Harvard, was a muralist, portraitist, and an Assistant Curator at the Metropolitan Museum of Art. I'm happy to know that my grandparents, father, and aunts were intelligent, good people, with strength, zest, and talents. They were far from perfect. I don't care.

Please don't feel threatened by my pride and excitement at integrating all the pieces of myself into one solid identity. Your parents and Dad's have been the foremost influences in forming my self-image. You and Dad made me competent to handle great difficulties. You also gave me the strength to enjoy being unique, instead of trying to be like everybody else.

I feel no conflict concerning my Jewish and non-Jewish relatives. I know who I am.

What I want is to be as free to talk with you about all the aspects of my life as you feel to talk about yours. We don't need to discuss my parentage and related matters constantly, but right now, I can't even broach the subject with you.

Yes, it's true that I strongly believe you should not have called my father "The Shvantz." If there's one thing that approach does not engender in a kid, it's security. The kid is not dumb enough to fool herself into believing that only her Dutch family imparted their characteristics to her.

I admit, I want to have this out in the open between us—not to hurt or reprimand you—but because it's such an important aspect of my life. Secrecy to the rest of the world is fine if that's what you want. But this secrecy among ourselves is built on unnecessary shame that has harmed all four of us.

Imagine how Neill felt when he learned about my father. He must have felt shock, confusion, disappointment, and maybe primarily—mistrust. I'm positive he didn't care that you'd been divorced. He only cared about the effect of the revelation on him. How could he trust anyone again if he couldn't trust his parents?

I first recognized your shame the day you were interviewed at the Holocaust Museum when you told me you were still ashamed of your first marriage. I was astonished and sad.

Mom, you should not feel any shame. Your first marriage was completely understandable. He was a handsome, smart man. He appeared to offer security. You were young, traumatized, afraid to be Jewish, and living in a new culture. Even if he'd been Jewish, the marriage wouldn't have worked. He came from a family where his father dominated his mother. He wasn't urban, intellectual, or interested in politics. He just wasn't for you. You didn't have enough experience to know that.

Based on your parents' close marriage and your mother's business, you had high ideals about marriage and family. And you wanted a career.

Through what you viewed as your stupid mistaken marriage, not only were you bearing the stigma of divorce, you also were a kid saddled with a kid. How could you get advanced education and hold down a job? How could you find a man who'd accept you and the kid? I think this predicament—which you felt you'd created for yourself—is what fuels your shame to this day, not the mere fact of the mistaken marriage itself. But you got yourself a wonderful husband (couldn't have been more perfect for you) and found me a wowzer of a father (besides being smart, nice, and completely loveable, he made Plasticine monkeys and told stories!)

Not only did you have a career, unlike most women, but you obtained your education under difficult circumstances: you worked in the daytime and studied at night in a cramped apartment full of people.

I've longed to say these things to you, not to hurt you, but to grow closer—and to heal.

Love,
Ingrid

MOM AND I WERE ensconced in the swivel rattan chairs at the breakfast table. The smell of coffee with chicory rose from our cups. I relished my early mornings with Mom when we visited, before the rest of the family emerged from the bedrooms. Dwayne and I had travelled down to Dallas with our son and daughter the night before.

"Is that college student you hired making life any easier for you?" she asked. An extension of our telephone conversations about juggling kids and work. She pushed the cheese board closer to me so I could cut some slices of gouda.

Before I could answer, she said, "I was very insecure as a young mother. I was all alone in a strange place without my parents, without any family nearby. I felt I needed to be strict."

This, I knew, was her apology for hitting me with the belt and smaller injustices.

"Remember you wouldn't let me cross the street by myself, even though all the other kids could?" I laughed—my acceptance of the apology and my private recognition of her terrible anxiety.

"Yah. I do remember." She laughed, too. We both sipped our coffee.

Mom put down her cup and looked at me. "Did I ever tell you that when I married Dad, Tante Sonja offered to keep you and raise you? I told Tante Sonja, 'Nothing doing!' I wanted you with me, and so did Dad."

I smiled and savored the message.

As much as I wanted her to acknowledge my letter, I wouldn't prod her—yet.

That afternoon, Mom and I stood in the white rope maze outside the IMAX theater at the science museum. Dad, Dwayne, and the kids were somewhere behind us. Buffered by strangers on all sides, Mom said to me, "He was not a bad man. I just didn't understand the culture in this country. We were too different from each other."

"That's right, Mom," I managed to say, as the waiting crowd began to surge into the movie theater. This response to the letter was all she managed to offer during our visit. I could wait.

I CALLED TO TELL MOM how much the four of us enjoyed the week with her and Dad.

"Don't feel sorry for me, Inky." That, I believed, was another reference to the letter—to my crying about her escape and maybe to my sorrow about her shame over the divorce.

"Oh, Mom, I love you."

"I appreciate your love so much you have no idea. And I appreciate the kind of human being you are. You're a better person than I am."

A better person than she is! That made me squirm. I had never heard her belittle herself—and to me. Why? Was she referring to the letter, to the way she'd made me feel by calling my father "The Shvantz"? I did not want an apology. I wanted to end the secrecy inside our family. Or was she referring to her general way of handling people versus mine?

She was clearly too uncomfortable to explain what she meant. And her discomfort fed mine. I could only say, "No, Mom, you're a good person."

"Ingrid, everyone has good parts in them and bad parts. You may not like the way I do things, but we'll just have to accept each other and get along."

This could refer to the typical mother daughter squabbles we'd had during the years or to the effects on me of how she handled the divorce.

Her vagueness didn't provide me the catharsis or the closeness I wanted. But I realized over time what my mother said to me in that conversation was way more than I should have expected.

5

LAYERS OF PAPERS—OLD CALENDARS, PAGES RIPPED FROM AN address book, black and white pictures of Mom, recipes jotted on lined notebook paper—spread across the kitchen counters and hung precariously over their edges. Pill bottles peeked from between the layers. I picked up a bottle here and there, read the label and for whom it was prescribed. I knew that this upheaval represented a state of mind, an inability to prioritize, organize, or process much of anything. This upheaval in the home of my once fastidious surgeon Dad who kept every instrument and anatomy book in its place and who planned out every operation and of my mother who had reviewed all the finances in Dad's office and supervised their private investments down to each interest and dividend payment, this upheaval confirmed why I'd come to drive them that day to the retirement community where they'd agreed to live—and why two months later, Dwayne and I would drive them around the back of the building to Memory Support.

Mom and I stood alone among the tilting piles.

Unable to admit I'd already lost my parents, I tried one more time. "Mom, there's only one thing I regret. I wish I could've talked to you openly about my father and the secrecy."

My mother replaced on the top of a pile whatever item she'd been examining. She looked at me. "Ingrid, I survived the Holocaust, and I had a good life. And you can have a good life, too." This issued out of the chaos of my mother's mind.

Of course, I could have a good life. I did have a good life.

But I understood. This was her final plea to let the subject drop.

I wanted something from her that she could never give—not only because she was wounded and still had nightmares about being chased by the Nazis—but because she was my mother.

The End

Afterword

THIS BOOK IS CREATIVE NONFICTION, WHICH MEANS I'VE CREATED scenes and dialogue to make the story more interesting. Most names were changed, because I did not seek permission to write about those individuals. However, everything in this book has a strong basis in reality. I knew most of my relatives mentioned in this book—as well as Marcie, her brother, and parents—for many years. Although I don't remember meeting Granddaddy and Aunt Kanka more than that one time in Crawfordsville, from pictures it's evident I did meet them and Aunt Mary Frances when I was too young to remember.

I drew from the following sources: family stories my parents and Tante Sonja shared throughout my life, the stories of her life that my mother poured into me, notes I wrote immediately after several conversations with my mother and on the flight back from North Carolina, extensive notes about my thoughts and fears related to contacting my father, my husband's photographs of my father and Dottie's home, all of the correspondence from my father, along with the pictures and newspaper clippings he sent, and years of letters and photographs saved by my parents and by Aunt Lippy, including letters among my father and his sisters which informed me of their personalities, family stories, and the language to use in dialogue.

All letters quoted in this book are from the originals, including carbon or computerized copies of my own letters. Aunt Lippy gave me her own poems, Aunt Kanka's book of poetry, and a detailed family genealogy researched by a member of my father's family. My mother made an album of items from their escape, their ship journey to Surinam, and her flights to Washington, D.C.

The Doll

The Doll

Magic Circles

I once heard a Yiddish writer describe magic circles in the air
with goats and rabbis and Shabbos candles
floating in them.
Pieces of his childhood, he said.
And afterwards I wept with a nostalgia that wasn't mine.
I wanted to be floating in a magic circle of my mother's life,
to make it whole again.

THE DOLL WAS PORCELAIN, HER SKIN AS UNBLEMISHED AND luminescent as a real child's, her cheeks as rosy as a baby's on a winter day, her hair and eyelashes soft and fine, not painted on or brittle like the hair on my dolls. I saw the doll for the first time when I was three and longed to hold her, feel her soft skin against my fingers, cup her cheek in my palm, kiss her. But when I asked, my mother refused.

"No, if you dropped her, she'd break. I'll let you hold her when you're older."

"Please, please, let me hold her," I begged.

"Not until you're older." She was adamant.

The doll was one of the few remnants of my mother's childhood. On her eighteenth birthday, she closed the door of her house behind her and with her mother and younger sister stole out of the Netherlands, each wearing as many dresses as possible layered beneath their coats. They walked on gold coins hidden in the hollow heels of their shoes.

In her arms, my mother carried a bag of tomatoes my grandmother—Moms—had purchased at the market early that morning. I heard about that bag for the first time when I was six. My mother was slicing tomatoes at the gray Formica table in our apartment.

"That bag became heavier and heavier as I walked," she said. "I kept begging Moms, *Please let me throw the bag away. I can't stand it anymore, it's so heavy.*"

"And did she let you?" I asked, to encourage her story telling.

"No. She said, *Sienie, that's our only food. I don't know when we'll get more, so be thankful you can carry it.*"

"Did you walk the whole way?"

"No. We took a train from The Hague to a Dutch farm house near the Belgian border. That was a big risk, because Jews weren't allowed on the trains. The Nazis checked every other train. They went through the cars looking at identification papers. We were lucky. They didn't check our train. We didn't have any papers. We'd torn up our identity cards marked *J* for *Jew*, and left without passports. They would have known we were Jews.

"Moms had found a *passeur* for us, a person who helped Jews escape from the Nazis. Tante Sonja and Uncle Rob left soon after their wedding, way before we did, because the Nazis were rounding up military age men. We planned to meet them in Nice. Moms paid the *passeur* to take us to Antwerp. Seventeen other people, friends of ours from The Hague, were escaping with the same *passeur*. We were all supposed to meet at the Dutch farm house. We traveled there in small groups. There was less chance of being noticed."

"Did everybody make it to the farmhouse?"

"They did. All seventeen of our friends showed up.

"From there, we had to walk across into Belgium because the Nazis checked all the trains at borders. Again, the *passeur* sent us in small groups. Moms, Tante Nannie, and I went together.

"We stayed off the roads. We walked right through the farmers' fields. When the three of us crossed into Belgium, a farmer was working in the field. He put his hoe on his shoulder and looked at us.

"You better turn back, he shouted. *Everyone sees what you're doing.*

"I was carrying that bag of tomatoes. *Dear God*, I whispered, *Please protect us. I haven't been able to eat kosher food. Please forgive me. If I survive, I promise I will eat only kosher food again."*

My mother had walked through a field, wearing all those dresses, and carrying a bag of tomatoes. For a moment I tried to think exactly how she'd felt when the farmer yelled at my mother, Moms, and Tante Nannie, but I pushed the thought away. I didn't want to know.

From my mother I learned it was possible to live in a house with many rooms, with wood paneled walls, and Persian carpets, with a servant who turned down the bed at night and put a warming brick at the bottom, who twisted yeast dough into *challahs* while orange peel and ginger lay waiting for the honey cake and the smell of chicken soup wended its way through the house. I learned it was possible to have all of that and to leave—to walk out wearing the dresses you could layer beneath your coat, close the front door, and never return. Not to that house, not to that street, not to that country.

And I learned that it was possible to have a father who loved you so much that even when he was tired he would play games with you after dinner for winnings of hazelnuts, engaging you in pretend combat so fierce it was clear nothing mattered to him more than you. I learned it was possible for that man—who once traded by dog sled in Siberia, who owned two movie theaters in The Hague, who allowed his wife to run her own business—to be struck down and die.

I learned these things in my crib. Fear and anger lived around its edges. They sprang at me in my mother's voice.

"The Nazis killed my father," she told me. "Those rotten Nazis killed my father."

The story of my mother's escape became the litany of my childhood. And she filled my childhood with stories of her childhood in The Hague.

The day my mother showed me the doll, when I was three years old, I was obsessed with holding her.

"Please, Mommy, *please*, let me play with her," I begged.

"No, you could break her. She's very fragile," she said again.

"Oh, Mommy, I'll be careful. I just want to hold her."

"Well . . . O.K."

She gave me the doll. The lighted face was in my hands. But the porcelain didn't feel the way it looked. The skin was hard and cool.

When my mother turned away, I smashed the doll on the floor. The body splintered. The head was the only part that did not break.

"How could you be so clumsy?" my mother screamed. "I told you to be careful. Why did I ever let you hold her!"

I cried. Did my mother cry, too? I don't remember. She picked up the head and all the other pieces. I didn't learn what she did with them until I was a teenager.

MY FIRST DAY OF SCHOOL, my mother didn't make me take the bus. I sat beside her on the cracked plastic seat of our Plymouth and heard about her school days. In the Netherlands, she told me, children came home from school for lunch.

"I danced into the dining room each day singing to my mother, I was so happy to see her."

She painted the scenes with vivid details, the red Persian carpet she danced across, the thick green pea soup she detested but that often waited in a large flowered soup tureen in the center of the dining room table.

My mother smiled at me beside her in the car.

"In the Netherlands," she continued, "there were different kinds of high schools. Mine was the best girls' school in The Hague. It was a school that led to university, for girls who wanted careers—much different from the high schools here. We took more subjects, and they were harder. My school was the equivalent of high school and college in this country."

I could hear the pride in her voice.

"I took fourteen subjects and had school six days a week. But, my parents made me stay home on *Shabbat*. I always studied ahead so I wouldn't fall behind from missing school on Saturday."

Our car rounded a corner, and I had my first glimpse of my elementary school. Beside me, my mother's tone changed.

"Of course," she said, as we pulled into the parking lot, "when the Nazis came, that was the first time I knew who the other Jews in my class were—when they made us wear the yellow stars. In my school, people didn't socialize by religion."

That first morning in my Texas elementary school, after I kissed my mother goodbye and climbed the dusty wooden steps of what I would learn to call the "shack," one of the many portables behind the brick school building, I was told to stand at attention beside my desk along with the other kids, while over the loudspeaker the voice of the principal led us in reciting what she called "The Lord's Prayer," to me a strange hodge podge of words that were clearly a Christian prayer.

Anger and shame coursed through me. Around me rose the other voices loud and clear along with the crisp firm voice of the principal coming through the loudspeaker. I stood, silent among them, staring at the newly washed blackboard and repeating the *Sh'ma*, the holiest Jewish prayer, over and over in my mind while very carefully moving my lips. A yellow star burned on my chest.

WHEN WE WENT SHOPPING, my mother bought me treats. Once, near a fabric shop she liked, she took me to a special candy store, a little place with green walls. The counter seemed to fill the store. Behind a pane of glass twice my height lay rows of different colored candies. It was almost impossible for me to choose between a marzipan strawberry and a miniature watermelon slice made of sugared coconut.

Finally, I chose the tiny melon slice, and as I carried the small white bag to the car, my mother recounted her own difficulties in choosing a treat when Moms took her shopping.

"I would stand for a long time, staring into a pickle barrel in my favorite store, trying to decide between a pickle or a big diamond shaped piece of *zoute drop*, salty licorice, that I'd hold in my hand and suck on for hours."

I kicked the gravel in the parking lot. Dust swirled into the air around me. I wanted to be left alone with my own candy and my own enjoyment.

I bit into the red crescent of my little watermelon slice. It tasted strongly of coconut.

"So, how's your candy?" my mother wanted to know as we climbed into the car.

"It's good. It's coconut."

Several times Dad had brought home a whole coconut from the grocery store. He took it out to the back step and cracked it with a hammer. It was exciting to look inside the brown hairy ball and see the white lining. He poured the milk into a cup for me to drink.

"I know you like coconut," my mother said as I took another bite of the tiny melon slice. "You and Dad. I can't look at coconut any more. All I had to eat in the southern part of France was coconut."

I didn't know then what had happened in the southern part of France, but as I learned more of her story, I could no longer stand the taste of coconut.

EVERY JEWISH HOLIDAY, my mother told me about hers. About the new dress Moms bought for her every *Rosh Hashona*, the holy Jewish New Year, a special dress of velvet and satin, and about "Pop," her father, praying in shul all day on *Yom Kippur*, the Day of Atonement.

Her descriptions of her family's *Sukkot* celebrations especially captured my imagination. My parents and I never built the booth to eat in or even celebrated the seven days that commemorate our wanderings in the desert. But every fall, I imagined the *sukkah* in my mother's tiny backyard illuminating the grass and bushes with candlelight from inside the walls of leaves and branches. And in my imagination, I would sing along, beating the rhythm on the linen covered table as my grandfather led songs inside that little booth where the smell of ripe fruit and cut leaves hung in the air.

And she'd told me about her childhood Sabbaths, about the cook's day long preparations, about the little *challah*, the braided egg bread, the cook made just for my mother, and about playing monopoly or card games with my grandfather after the Friday night dinner.

She'd also told me about her own job before *Shabbat*. Every Friday before sundown, she'd torn enough toilet paper for the whole family to use until sundown on Saturday, because tearing toilet paper on the Sabbath was forbidden work. My mother said she'd dreaded the job, but loved *Shabbat* once it settled over their home every Friday at sundown.

One Friday afternoon, I slammed through the back door of our apartment into the narrow kitchen, wiping the grit from my outdoor adventures onto my jeans. My mother stood at the counter melting the bottoms of the white *Shabbat* candles so they would sit firmly in the candlesticks. I looked up at her serious face as she held the flame to the bottom of a dripping candle. Her eyes on the candles, she recounted another memory of her Sabbaths.

"The best part of *Shabbat* when I was a child was going to my grandparents' house. Every Saturday after your grandfather came home from praying in the synagogue, we walked to their house. We didn't ride our bicycles on *Shabbat*. Your grandfather led the way in his best suit and the black silk top hat he'd worn to synagogue that morning, next to him, Moms in her newest dress. Tante Nannie, Tante Sonja, and I wore our best dresses.

"*Opa*, my grandfather, always met us at the door. He hugged us and gave us big kisses on both cheeks. Then, he'd turn to me and my sisters, raise his eyebrows, put one finger on his lips, and before Oma, my grandmother, could call us to lunch, he'd sneak us down into the cellar where great big *wursts* hung on ropes from the ceiling. The cellar was a dark place that smelled like mold and salami. To me and my sisters it was very exciting to sneak down there with Opa. He'd always whisper that Oma would be angry if she knew we were down there. Then he'd take a pen knife out of his pocket and cut us each a piece of the *wurst* we picked.

"*Would* your Oma have been angry if she knew you were down there?" I asked.

"No," my mother laughed. "She did know. It was just a game Opa played that she'd be angry. He loved to kid around. He made the same jokes every *Shabbat*, and we loved it.

"It made me so secure to have my grandparents nearby. I knew they loved me."

My mother stared past the candles, now in their candlesticks. She was back in that world, and I had followed her there.

I understood how my mother felt about her family. I felt the same way about mine. The three of us, my parents and I, formed the essential unit of my life. Everything else hung at the periphery.

When I came home from school, my mother asked about everything I did and listened to everything I said. Even when I told her stories like The Gingerbread Man that went on and on forever, she stood in the kitchen cooking and chuckled at all the right places.

I knew I was the most important person in her life just like she was in mine.

MY MOTHER FOLDED an edge of my sheet under the mattress. "Now you do it," she said. I folded the other side under. I was seven, old enough to make my own bed, she'd said. While she taught me, I discovered that the reasons for making my bed were different from the reasons for other children.

"After Moms, Tante Nannie, and I snuck across the Belgian border, we walked through farm fields at night," she said, as I tucked in a corner. "In the daytime we slept in the unmade beds of Belgian farmers, at places where the *passeur* had arranged for us to stay. Some of the beds were still warm from the people who'd just slept in them. It made me feel so dirty.

"To this day, I can't stand the sight of an unmade bed."

I helped my mother pull up the blanket.

"In Antwerp, we met up with the *passeur* before he left us. Only nine in our group of twenty made it. Moms, Tante Nannie, and I stayed with my aunt and uncle and their daughter, Miriam, while Moms looked for another *passeur* to take us to the southern part of France. We stayed in their apartment for four days. It was too dangerous to go out. There were Nazi soldiers everywhere. Finally, a friend of my uncle found a *passeur* for us."

My mother and I both grabbed an end of the bedspread and pulled it over the pillow. Then she showed me how to crease the spread and tuck a bit under the pillow.

"Moms begged my aunt and uncle to go with us, but they refused to leave. The day after we left, the Nazis took them to a concentration camp."

My mother had never told me more about the camps than *You never came back.* But her tone said more.

I put my stuffed animal cocker spaniel on top of the bedspread.

"Your Jewish name, Miriam, is in memory of my cousin."

At that moment, I was very grateful for my other name, the one I'm known by every day, grateful that I could hide from this memory.

WE WERE DOWNTOWN shopping one Saturday. My mother had just decided to stop for lunch. We waited at a street corner for the light to change. The sun glared off the pavement, and she fanned at the muggy Houston air with her shopping list.

"This heat is *awful.* When we first moved to Houston, Dad and I came downtown to handle some business at the bank. I fainted on the sidewalk. In the Netherlands the weather is cool and rainy. If someone had told me when I was a girl that someday I'd be living in Texas, I would have had to look it up on a map."

The light changed. I followed her into the department store to the lunch counter and climbed onto the stool beside hers. I knew we'd have the same lunch we always had there, a cup of vegetable soup and a napoleon.

This rectangular sweet, constructed of thin layers of crispy pastry and layers of custard, was my mother's favorite.

"It reminds me of the pastries we had in the Netherlands," she said every time we ate at that counter.

I cut the first bite of my napoleon, sticking the points of the fork straight down into the thinly iced top, just as my mother had taught me, when suddenly—in the din of that American lunch counter, the clatter of the plates of burgers and fries that passed around us, the shouted orders from the waitress to the cook, the roar of the milkshake machine—my mother asked, "Did I tell you what else Moms bought along with that bag of tomatoes I carried into Belgium?"

I shook my head. The piece of pastry hung on my fork.

"Remember the day we left the Netherlands was my eighteenth birthday?"

I nodded my head and began to eat.

"Well, Moms felt terrible that she couldn't give me a present. So, early in the morning when she went to the market to get food for our escape, she looked for something special to celebrate my birthday.

"While she was gone, Tante Nannie and I were in our rooms getting ready. I put on the dresses I'd chosen. One on top of the other. Then I checked through my overcoat to be sure I had everything. We needed our coats even though it was summer. I'd sewn a pocket inside to carry a few things, a little book about Van Gogh, some pencils and paper.

"We were lucky to have real leather shoes. As soon as they'd invaded, the Nazis had taken all the leather shoes—and everything else good that people needed. The leather shoes we wore that day were part of a big inventory Moms had hidden in the attic which she used as the warehouse for the shoe store. The Nazis never found them.

"Those shoes in the attic helped save our lives. When Moms decided we would escape, she sold them on the black market for money instead of ration cards. A Nazi officer discovered what she was doing and offered to buy her entire stock for a very good price. She knew this man and decided to take the risk. He could have turned her in, but he gave her the money. That's how she got enough money to pay the *passeurs*. They charged thousands of dollars a person. Most of the money from the shoes she changed into gold. That gold paid for our escape.

"The shoes I put on that morning had hollow heels filled with gold coins. During our whole escape, we never took off those shoes. We even slept in them.

"When she returned from the market, Moms called upstairs to Tante Nannie and me that she had a treat for us. We hadn't had many treats because the Nazis had taken everything. So we were very excited.

"On the dining room table on our best china, Moms had placed three peaches. They were the most delicious looking food I'd seen in ages."

"Just as delicious as these napoleons?"

My mother hesitated for a second.

"Yes," she laughed. "Just as delicious.

"Moms and Tante Nannie sang the Dutch birthday song to me, *Lang zal ze leven*, long shall she live. Then we ate the peaches. When we finished, we cut the yellow stars off our coats and left."

I'd managed to eat my entire napoleon as my mother spoke. I'd made a game of trying to cut exactly the same sized piece each time I sank my fork into the layers of the pastry. That way, I couldn't feel anything.

MY MOTHER WAS TEACHING me to knit. I was knitting a stole for my doll, a long narrow wrap to throw around her shoulders. I liked the click of the needles. My mother sat beside me knitting a sweater she planned to cover with sequins.

"I learned to knit in elementary school," she said. But then she began to recall other memories.

"It was the *passeur's* job to tell us which train to take from Antwerp to Brussels. Of course, there was no guarantee. The Nazis could have checked any one of them. We would have been discovered without papers and sent to a camp. I was trembling on the train. There were Nazi soldiers at every train station. I was scared every time the train stopped somewhere that the Nazis were getting on. I was scared every time someone walked past our compartment."

I had to watch every stitch of my knitting, but I looked up for a moment to find my mother's intense green eyes on me as her needles clicked.

"When we arrived in Brussels, the new *passeur* led us from the train station in Brussels into the busiest streets of the city. There were Nazi soldiers on every corner standing at attention in their green uniforms. I was sure they were watching me, even though the *passeur* led us down busy streets among many people, some on foot like us, many on bicycles. Then, suddenly, the *passeur* was gone. He'd taken us into the middle of the city and lost us in the street. We'd already paid him to take us all the way from Antwerp to the southern part of France. He had our money, but he didn't want to take the risk.

"Right there in the street, with the soldiers all around us, Moms stopped a man who was wearing a Jewish star. She whispered to him what had happened. He let us sleep on the floor in his apartment and helped us find another *passeur*. We must have stayed with this man two or three days."

For a moment, the only sound was the clicking of our knitting needles.

"From Brussels, we were planning to go to Nice in the southern part of France. The Nazis had already taken over the northern part of France, but not the south. So, we thought we'd be safe there. The southern part, Vichy France, was controlled by General Petain and his friend Mr. Laval who set up a government in the city of Vichy. We soon discovered they weren't much better than Hitler.

"To get to Nice, we had to take two trains. One to the demarcation line between occupied France and Vichy France—somewhere between Dijon and Lyon—and the other train from Lyon to Nice. The Nazis were watching the demarcation line very carefully. So we had to walk across, all the way to Lyon in the south.

"Again, we walked at night and slept during the day in farm houses the *passeur* had arranged. We walked through farmer's fields and even crossed streams. We were a mess by the time we reached Lyon.

"All the way from Brussels to Lyon I was terrified that the Nazis would find me. I was afraid they'd board a train and ask for my papers, I was afraid to hear a knock on the door in every farm house, afraid of every movement and sound at night in the fields. One night I saw fireflies and thought it was Nazis coming toward us carrying flashlights."

My hands were clenched, and I held my breath. My knitting rested in my lap, abandoned.

My mother continued, "We did reach Lyon. We stopped there to go to the Dutch Consulate. Moms hoped we could get papers.

"We thought the Dutch consul believed Moms' story that we were Protestants who left the Netherlands quickly without papers because a Nazi soldier was too interested in me. He gave us papers. In the places for religion, he wrote *Protestant* and he misspelled our last name. He also told us that as Dutch citizens we could go to Surinam, a Dutch colony, and since we had a country to go to, we could get transit visas across Spain and Portugal.

"After the war, we learned that this Dutch consul was a Jewish man named Sally Noach. When he believed people were Jewish refugees, he wrote another religion on the papers he gave them. And he wrote a name that didn't sound so Jewish."

That summer, I went to Connecticut to stay with Tante Nannie and Uncle Hal. Moms took my cousin and me to New York City on the New Haven Railroad. It was my first time on a train. Moms told us about Radio City Music Hall, our destination that day, the bakery we'd visit afterwards, and the pastries we'd bring back with us.

"Pastries with marzipan and chocolate?" I asked.

"Of course," she assured me with a wide smile.

I'd been too busy talking with Moms to notice the conductor collecting tickets until he stood beside me. I looked up, startled—and despite my certain knowledge it was only fantasy—the conductor in his uniform became a Nazi soldier not checking tickets—but identity papers. And I succumbed to the fear that he would yell "Jew!" and grab me.

I managed to hold out my ticket, but as the conductor moved away, I gripped the edge of my seat and only pretended to laugh at a joke my cousin was telling.

MY MOTHER WAS DRIVING to the tennis lessons she'd decided I should take the summer after fifth grade. I was watching dust moats float past the windshield when she broke the silence.

"My father would have liked playing tennis," she said. "He was such an active man. When he was young, before he met Moms, he traded by dog sled in Siberia."

I'd only seen my grandfather in pictures. In them, my grandfather, a man with broad cheeks, a thick dark moustache, and intelligent eyes, was always dressed in a double breasted suit and stood sedately smiling beside Moms. It was difficult to imagine that man seated behind a team of huskies, skimming across a white landscape. It was easier to think of him in the other roles my mother had so frequently described, walking to synagogue in his top hat, giving out money before *Shabbat* to the poor, standing in one of his movie theaters, playing monopoly and card games with my mother and my aunts at the *Shabbat* table.

She'd told me once the Nazis beat him the day they confiscated his theaters. As she spoke of him now, I wondered if that was how he'd died. My mother answered the unspoken question.

"My father had a heart attack that day the Nazis hit him in one of his movie theaters," she said. "It was in the evening, during the curfew. For hours that night, Moms was upstairs taking care of my father, and I was on the phone downstairs in the shoe store—so my father couldn't hear—calling doctors. But no one would come. The Jewish doctors were afraid to go out during the curfew. If a soldier stopped them on the street, who knew what would happen. The gentile doctors wouldn't help a Jew. *Are you Jewish?* they asked me. *Oh, I can't help you*, they said.

"In the morning when the curfew was over, a Jewish doctor came. But it was too late."

And then my mother's eyes darkened.

"The Nazis killed my father," she spit out bitterly. "Those rotten Nazis." The refrain I'd heard so many times. The core of her bitterness. No other loss—of her home, her country, her culture— was as searing. She'd said it so many times.

"If only I hadn't lost my father. . ."

I hated them, too, those Nazis. And I wanted to protect her, and protect myself, from the pain they'd inflicted, from the pain of losing someone so special.

It's too late, I thought as I crossed the blazing pavement of the parking lot, headed toward the tennis courts. I knew if I lost any of my relatives, I'd be devastated. But already I was hardening myself against other attachments that could hurt me as much.

WHEN I WAS IN FIRST and second grade, my mother bought me embroidered sweaters and blouses, until I convinced her not to.

"This is how European girls dress," she told me with each purchase. In photographs Moms had retrieved from The Hague after the war, I'd seen the kind of dresses my mother and aunts had worn in the Netherlands. They have puffy sleeves, embroidery, little collars at the neck, and sashes.

It took more convincing to get rid of my hairdo, the braids with bows on each end. By seventh grade, I wore clothes like my classmates' and labored every morning over a version of the bouffant hairdo Jackie Kennedy had made popular.

Until my Bat Mitzvah.

Several months before the date, my mother met me at the door after school, her eyes shining.

"I bought you an outfit for your Bat Mitzvah. Wait until you see it. It's gorgeous!"

Maybe she thought I'd be relieved. It was well known in our family that I detested shopping, which was a big disappointment to my mother. Our shopping expeditions usually ended in exasperation on her part because I wouldn't even look through the racks, and anger on mine because I couldn't stand having her nag me to look.

Instead of feeling relief at being spared a jaunt through the stores with my mother, I was furious that she'd chosen what I was to wear on my first foray in front of so many people on a day I thought of as *my* special day.

"Do you want to see what I bought you?"

"Okay," I responded glumly.

She led me into her bedroom and took the outfit out of her closet. It was white organdy. Organdy. Wasn't that what old ladies' curtains were made of? A skirt and a blouse. A great big gathered skirt, about mid-calf length. And a blouse with white puffy sleeves, a high-necked collar, and embroidery.

"Do you like it?" A satisfied smile creased the skin around my mother's eyes.

I screwed up my courage.

"Not really," I said quietly.

"Ach. It's beautiful. What don't you like?"

"The puffy sleeves."

"They look so nice. Is that all?"

I wanted to say, "Mom, I don't like any of it. I hate organdy. It looks like old ladies' curtains. I can't stand puffy sleeves and embroidery and high necked little collars. And I don't want a skirt and blouse. No one dresses like this anymore!"

But all I said was, "I wanted a dress. Something . . . stylish."

"This *is* stylish. I got it at Neimans. I think it's so pretty."

I dared a little further, "Mom, I wanted to pick it. Why don't we take this back, and I'll go with you to pick something.

"I got it on sale. They won't take it back. You'll wear it, and you'll look beautiful."

I wore it. In 1960, I looked like a Dutch kid right out of the 1930's.

NICE. AS A TEENAGER I read books about artists who reveled in the light of the Riviera. I read uncomprehending. For me, there can never be sunlight on the Riviera.

For nearly two months in a hotel in Nice, the Garden Hotel, where honeymoons and sex trysts took place at other times in history, my mother with Tante Nannie and Moms—then the sole survivors of the group of twenty with whom they'd left the Netherlands—waited to get transit visas across Spain to Portugal.

"They came every night," my mother told me, "the Vichy police. We heard their boots on the circular stairs near our room. Very loud. I always thought, *They're coming for me.* Then we heard the screams of other Jews being pulled from their rooms and down that circular staircase. The screams of those other Jews I will never forget as long as I live."

Every night, these accomplices of Hitler banged on the door to the room where those three women stood.

"Any Jews in this room?" the uniformed figures shouted as they looked under the bed and into the closets. And every night, Moms showed their "Protestant" papers from the Dutch consul in Lyon, their savior, Sally Noach.

"As soon as they saw those papers, they always apologized for bothering us," my mother said.

On July 2, 1942, twelve days before my mother left the Netherlands—completely unknown to Moms—the Vichy government decided to meet the Nazi demand for Jews by turning over all Jewish refugees who made it into the unoccupied part of France. French born Jews would remain a little longer under the protection of the Vichy government. In the month before my mother arrived in Nice, the Vichy government handed the Nazis fifteen thousand Jewish refugees.[1] Vichy's contribution to The Holocaust, that carefully planned, industrialized genocide of the Jewish people. There, in those facts is the reality of my mother's fears and the reprieve from her shame at being rendered special— yet powerless—by her "Protestant" papers, while those other Jews were pulled down the stairs.

From my mother, I gained strength. Nothing that happened to me was as bad as what had happened to her. When I experienced my ordinary sorrows, I knew that despite them, I could go back to my home with my parents and sleep in my own bed.

EVENTUALLY I HEARD how my mother was reunited with her doll. After she came to the United States, Moms returned to The Hague to reclaim property she'd left with the neighbors. The faces of the husband and wife were grim with surprise when they saw her at their doorstep, but they invited her in. She walked on the dark reds and deep blues of her own Persian carpets as they led her into their home, offered her tea, and politely inquired about her escape. Moms had no energy to fight about carpets. She asked for the suitcases filled with photographs and was relieved when the couple handed them over.

---

[1] Lucy S. Dawidowicz, *The War Against the Jews 1933-1945*, 10th ed. (New York: Bantam Books, 1986), 362.

Moms brought back the stock and bond certificates she'd hidden in the linings of those suitcases. She also brought back the photographs and my mother's doll.

After Moms' trip, my mother had shown me the doll, and the memory never left me of my mother's scream when I dropped it.

AT AGE FOURTEEN, I read *Exodus*—my first explicit knowledge of the ghettos and of what had happened in the camps. I knew the crying would come, so I waited until my parents went out one Sunday afternoon to read the part about the Warsaw Ghetto uprising and Dov, the young boy, crawling through the sewers. I sat on my bed and cried and writhed and grabbed my arms around myself, tangled in my mother's pain. It didn't help. I couldn't cry the feelings away.

Why did she have to tell me? Why did it have to happen? Why was she my mother? It meant always knowing her terror, her searing pain. My only chance at happiness was trying to forget, because I could not stand what I would have to feel if I did not stuff complete recognition of her anguish deep down inside me.

The summer after college, my Israeli cousin's tour company took me to Kibbutz Yad Mordechai's memorial for the Warsaw Ghetto. From the glaring sunlight, we entered the semidarkness of a small building. The walls were hung with photographs, and my eyes adjusted to my first encounters with the skeletons of the Holocaust: the hollow eyes of people huddled on floors in small rooms, the bodies flopped onto wooden carts, the fighters in the uprising. In the darkness, I put on my sunglasses and wept silently.

I thought about my mother standing in her kitchen on the flagstone floor, the walnut paneled walls sheltering her from the Texas sun. Encased again in a home where a silver cookie jar stands on a glass table above a Persian carpet, still, she often trembled in darkness, feeling as shelterless as when she had entered the darkness wrapped in her warmest clothes.

I carried that darkness with me.

KUBY'S, A EUROPEAN delicatessen my mother had discovered, became one of our favorite lunch places when I was in high school. We would each have a bowl of lentil soup and share a Lebanon baloney sandwich. That smoky *wurst* reminded my mother of the *wursts* that had hung in her grandfather's cellar. If we were lucky, Mr. Kuby would have received a shipment of Dutch salty licorice. Mom and I would buy a box of that *zoute drop* packaged in rolls like lifesavers. We could go through a roll or two for dessert while we talked.

I heard the Marseilles story at Kuby's. We were well into our first roll of *zoute drop* when our conversation drifted to the topic.

"When we got to Nice," she began. "Tante Sonja and Uncle Rob were already there waiting for us. Remember, they'd left way before we did, because the Nazis were rounding up military age men.

"We were hoping to go with them to Switzerland. You couldn't get into Switzerland legally because the Swiss weren't taking any Jewish refugees. So, you had to go over the mountains. But we learned from talking to other Jewish refugees that even in summer there was snow, and many people lost their lives. Also we heard that you had to make it a certain number of feet over the border before the Swiss found you or they'd throw you out and you'd have to climb back over the Alps. We decided not to try.

"We decided to follow the Dutch consul's advice and try to get to Surinam. We applied by mail to the Spanish and Portuguese consulates for visas to cross into Spain and Portugal. In October, we got the visas. But Franco had an agreement with Hitler that no men of military age were allowed into Spain. We couldn't get Uncle Rob a transit visa through Spain.

"Moms sent Tante Sonja ahead to Spain with a group of Dutch refugees sponsored by the Dutch consulate. Moms gave Uncle Rob money to bribe someone at the Spanish consulate in Marseilles. He would go alone, she'd decided, while she headed to Perpignan near the Spanish border with me and Tante Nannie.

"But I had another idea. I insisted on going with Uncle Rob. I'd heard about a man at the Spanish consulate who gave papers to women he liked the looks of. I decided to flirt with him. Tante Sonja had already burned a hole in Uncle Rob's passport with a cigarette to blot out his birth date. We thought that might help, too.

"When we arrived in Marseilles, Uncle Rob and I found a room in a hotel. I'll never forget the first night there. The room had only one bed, so Uncle Rob and I had to share it. Uncle Rob lay down and fell right asleep. But the minute I got into the bed, I was bitten all over by lice. I jumped off the bed and tried to sleep in a chair but couldn't. All night long I was scratching myself and listening to Uncle Rob's snoring and the thunder from a big storm outside.

"My flirting didn't help. Neither did the cigarette burn. The Spanish Consulate refused to give Uncle Rob a transit visa. Every night I was on the phone with Moms. And after a few days, she told me to come to the border because the Nazis were invading the southern part of France any day.

"So I left Uncle Rob in Marseilles and met Moms and Tante Nannie in Perpignan. From there, we took a train through the Pyrenees into Spain. Crowds of cheering people met our train at the first stop inside the border. The Dutch consul also met our train, and I asked him why they were cheering. He told me the Nazis had invaded the southern part of France while we were traveling through the Pyrenees.

"When our train reached Barcelona, Tante Sonja was waiting at the station. She had met every train from France since she'd arrived—waiting for Uncle Rob. When she saw that he wasn't with us, she cried. She was sure she would never see him again now that the Nazis had invaded."

My mother began peeling the wrapper off another roll of *zoute drop*.

"But Uncle Rob persevered with the Spanish Consulate in Marseilles. He gave them the money and got the visa. Uncle Rob took the last train into Spain before the Nazis closed the border."

She offered me the roll of *drop*. I shook my head.

"Flirting," my mother had said. With a man she'd heard granted favors to women he liked. That had to mean more than just standing beside Uncle Rob and smiling while Uncle Rob spoke to the man. My mother, at age eighteen, must have tried to get his attention, tried to talk to the man alone. Did she hope he'd ask her out? Did he? I refused to think any farther than that. I looked at my mother. Her dark brown hair that had once brushed her shoulders now framed her face. Her high cheeks were crimson, though she wore no makeup. Dad told me that when they met she was the most beautiful woman he'd ever seen.

At that moment, at the table in Kuby's, I felt completely separated from my mother, removed from her the same way I'd felt as a kid when I watched her doing business at the bank and her face changed into that stern, pulled-down-chin look. As a child I'd known I was seeing her in a world she inhabited without me, in a world where she was competent and I was not; and I'd felt estranged.

As she spoke about Marseilles, I was seeing her as a woman, not as my mother, but as a flirtatious, sexual being with bravery and cunning—even if her ploys hadn't gained her what she wanted.

Fury rose inside me.

Why anger, I asked myself. It was so wrong, so unfair, so selfish. How could I be angry? She was the one who'd lost everything—her father, her home, her education. She was the one who'd lived in terror for so many months. She was the one who had to try to con that man to save my uncle.

I wasn't angry because the story separated her from me—but because I was jealous. She was the star. She was the hero. How could anything I ever did match what she'd gone through—what she'd done to go through it? My mother's life had cheated me. Because of her loss, her deprivation, I chafed against exactly the type of life she was ripped out of. Because she had survived, I could not accept myself. I'd never suffered.

I could drag myself, dwarfed by my backpack, tent, and sleeping bag, up steep mountain trails. I could wake up at six every morning for long bike rides before school and live on starvation diets. I could apply to a college three thousand miles away and live alone in a big city and travel alone on the other side of the globe. I could stay up nights plodding through law books to get a J.D. and maybe even a tax master's. But every challenge I could ever face would be a contrivance. Everything I could ever do would be self-imposed, artificial. I could spend my whole life trying to survive the Holocaust. But I never would.

THE NAZIS WERE IN the southern part of France, and my family had barely escaped into Spain. They were saved.

They crossed from Spain into Portugal and, in Lisbon, boarded the S.S. Nyassa, a Portuguese ship arranged by the Joint Distribution Committee with the Dutch government-in-exile in London for Dutch Jewish refugees. Their destination was Paramaribo, the capital of the then Dutch colony, Surinam. For nearly three weeks, outcasts on the ocean, more homeless than an American asleep on a grate, these refugees headed to an unknown place within five degrees of the equator. They'd left their homes, their schools, their jobs, their belongings, and their cold, rainy climate. They'd moved in terror every step of the way that had led them to that ship where they now huddled, not quite sure what had happened to them or where they were going.

When they reached the Caribbean, one sun flecked day a Nazi U-boat surfaced beside the Portuguese ship. Nazi soldiers climbed aboard, randomly grabbed as many passengers as they could, and scurried them down into the depths of their submarine. My mother, Moms, my aunts and my uncle were not on deck during the raid.

The Dutch flag was flying over the harbor in Paramaribo. My mother, along with all the other grateful Dutch Jews, cried and sang the Dutch national anthem as their boat docked. The Dutch governor knew Jewish refugees were coming, and he was ready for them.

"He had built a camp for us, surrounded by fences and barbed wire—with guards," my mother told me. "The women were separated from the men and shuffled into big rooms full of cots. We had work duties. Moms, Tante Nannie, and I had kitchen duties."

My mother had been telling me her stories while I helped her unpack groceries. She had seen mangoes in the supermarket that morning and brought one home for me to try. Now, she picked up the mango.

"I ate mangoes for the first time in Surinam," she said. "I want to teach you how to eat them." She peeled the skin into a long spiral that fell away from the juicy yellow flesh onto the plate. She continued to talk about Surinam as she sliced the flesh.

"I lived in Surinam a year and seven months, six months of it in that camp. A Dutch Jewish teacher offered to tutor me and Tante Nannie so we could earn our degrees. You remember I was in a girls' school in The Hague that led to university before the Nazis forced us to attend a school for Jews. Tante Nannie was in the same girls' school. We didn't earn our degrees in the Netherlands before our escape. This teacher and his wife, Maurits and Annie Cardozo, had no children of their own. They asked Moms if Tante Nannie and I could live with them. Moms let us live with the Cardozos so that we could get out of that camp. The Cardozos lived in a house on stilts at the edge of the jungle."

My mother offered me the mango slices. I had never tasted fruit so sweet.

"Uncle Rob was taken into the Dutch military in Surinam. The Dutch government in Surinam gave him and Tante Sonja their own house. Moms went to live with them."

As I savored each slice of my first mango, my mother told me about the suffocating heat in Surinam, the dirt paths instead of sidewalks, the snake she found one morning wrapped around the handles of her bicycle where she parked it under the Cardozos' house, and the intelligent, kind Cardozos.

Instead of the fear I heard in her voice when she spoke about her escape and the U-boat, anger overshadowed everything she said about Surinam. Anger that the governor of Surinam, part of her own Dutch government, had stuck her, a Dutch citizen, in that camp.

I picked up the large flat pit of the mango and tore off the remaining flesh with my teeth, just as my mother had instructed.

While studying for her degree with Maurits Cardozo, my mother began to work for the Dutch Government in Surinam. When she earned her degree, the Dutch government-in-exile offered her a job as a statistician at the Dutch embassy in Washington, D.C. Three weeks after her twentieth birthday, two years after she'd walked away from her home in The Hague, my mother hugged Moms, Tante Nannie, Tante Sonja, Uncle Rob, and the Cardozos and boarded an airplane. She entered the United States on a diplomatic visa. My mother arrived in Washington,

D.C. with a small suitcase of personal items, one dress, forty dollars, and a pin Moms had an artisan make for my mother's twentieth birthday. It was a leaf of finely wrought brass dipped in a layer of gold from one of the coins that remained in a heel of Moms' shoes.

A year later, when Tante Nannie earned her degree, my mother found her a job at the Dutch Embassy in Washington. Moms, Tante Sonja, and Uncle Rob had to find a sponsor to put up bond for them, so they could move to the United States.

THE MORNING OF MY eighteenth birthday, the Texas sun poked long white fingers between my bedroom curtains. I stretched and thought, *On Mom's eighteenth birthday she began the escape.*

I leaned over the edge of my bed to pull open the curtains when my mother burst into the room.

"Happy Birthday!" she sang. She always greeted me that way on my birthday. In the Netherlands, birthdays were very important. The birthday person's place at the breakfast table was surrounded by cards and little presents. On their birthdays, school children brought sweets to school for their friends, and adults invited their friends to share pastries.

My mother sat on the edge of my bed and hugged me.

"This is an important birthday," she said. "Eighteen years old. On my eighteenth birthday, we began our escape." And then she launched into the story of her preparations that morning and Moms' gift of the peaches.

I didn't interrupt to tell her I'd heard it all before. She wasn't speaking for my benefit. She was speaking for her own. As if she were still incredulous at what had happened. As if repeating it all could somehow erase it. As if reciting the litany of how she was wronged could somehow bring some kind of justice.

"Did I tell you," she said, "that the day after we left, early in the morning, the Nazis came to our house with a truck to get us? Moms learned that from the neighbors when she went back after the war. We left way too late. We were lucky to get away. If we had left earlier like Tante Sonja and Uncle Rob, our trip wouldn't have been so dangerous."

The doorbell interrupted, and my mother went to answer it. I waited, assuming the early morning caller was a delivery man from the dry cleaners. When my mother didn't return, I crept down the hall, curious.

A strange woman stood in the doorway talking to my mother who now held a brown grocery bag. As I approached, my mother turned.

"Come meet our new neighbor. She just moved here from Georgia, and she's brought us some Georgia peaches!"

Our neighbor must have been gratified by the excitement in my mother's voice. My mother and I caught each other's eyes as she handed me the brown paper bag.

I took it to the kitchen, and still in my pajamas, sat at the breakfast table, resting one bare foot on the rattan base and another on the flagstone floor. In my hand, I held a peach bigger than my fist, almost entirely yellow and a bit too fuzzy, not as delicate a specimen as I imagined my mother having eaten.

I bit through the skin and juice trickled down my chin. The appearance of this bag of peaches on my eighteenth birthday didn't surprise me.

WE SPENT HOURS TOGETHER in the kitchen, baking, my mother and I. She taught me to make the European pastries she longed for, cream puffs, linzer tortes, Black Forest cakes. Her Black Forest cake was the most difficult, requiring a dozen eggs and delicate skill. The whites had to be separated without a trace of yolk, beaten, and once frothy, spread onto brown paper and placed into the oven so quickly that they turned to a thick crunchy meringue and not flat, clear brittle. My mother prided herself in always achieving the meringue, though a friend of hers sometimes lost several dozen eggs trying.

One Saturday when I was in high school, my mother gave me a lesson in making Black Forest cakes. She'd taught me when I was six or seven how to crack an egg and separate the white from the yolk. Now, standing in our kitchen with its walnut paneling and recessed lighting, my mother entrusted the entire dozen eggs to my separating skills. I hit the first egg on the side of the bowl, and she smiled approvingly.

"Moms never cooked with me," she said. "She never cooked anything in our house. She didn't even boil water. She told your grandfather before they got married that she wanted servants in the house so she could work in her own business. She went to a special school to learn how to handle servants."

I cracked and separated as my mother told these familiar stories.

"All through my childhood, Fannie lived in our house in a room right beside the kitchen. When I came downstairs for breakfast, I saw her false teeth still frozen into the glass of water she'd left on the window sill at night.

"All the tradesmen came to our door in horse drawn wagons— the baker, the grocer, the butcher. When the butcher came, Tante Nannie, Tante Sonja, and I snuck down the stairs to watch Fannie flirt with him. Fannie really liked that butcher. She would blush and become all flustered when she saw him. We thought it was so funny. Of course, if she ever caught us watching her, she was terribly angry."

While I added sugar to the egg whites and beat them to a froth, my mother flattened a brown paper bag onto a cookie sheet. Together we spread the stiffened egg whites across the paper to form one big rectangle.

"We're a good team," my mother said. We laughed in camaraderie as we each held a side of the cookie sheet and slid it into the oven.

We would wait until the meringue was baked and cool to melt the chocolate glaze and whip the cream that formed the top layer of the pastry.

"Come. Sit down," my mother said. "We've earned a cup of tea."

I followed her to the table where a picture window looked out onto her garden. She poured tea into the fluted porcelain cups she insisted on using for even the most casual occasions. I'd always loved these days when we baked and drank tea. These were our best times together. But all afternoon, though I'd felt so keenly my friendship with my mother, I'd also felt myself drawing away as she told her stories.

I understood and respected and was even thankful for her compulsion to recreate her childhood. But I didn't want to hear about it anymore.

THE SUMMER AFTER I graduated from college, I visited my mother's street in The Hague. In the dim light, I walked between the tall row houses built above each family's shop and remembered my mother telling me that she could easily see from her front window into the front window of the neighbor directly across the street. At my mother's address, I stopped.

I stood before the window of what had once been Moms' shoe store. Above it was the house I'd walked through as I'd listened to my mother's stories. I looked at the store front and tried to peer inside. But the window was glossy and dark. It blocked my view and threw back a reflection. I stared for some moments before I understood the reflection was mine. I had expected it to be my mother's.

A HIGH SCHOOL WEEKEND of reading a novel and sharing pizza and a movie with a friend. My parents had gone to a medical convention in San Antonio. Late Sunday night, my mother and I sat in the kitchen talking about our weekends.

"The first night in San Antonio," she confided. "I had a nightmare."

I looked up from my milky tea.

"I dreamed that in the middle of the night, I heard loud footsteps coming down the hall to our hotel room. I heard banging on the door. Nazi soldiers burst into our room and shouted, *Sienie Goudsmit! We missed you in Europe. So we've come for you here.*" She laughed a little as if to lighten the atmosphere after such a stark confession that more than twenty years later the girl who had escaped could never escape her fear of being discovered on a train, in a farm house, in a field, on a street, in a hotel—and sent to a concentration camp.

A FEW MONTHS BEFORE COLLEGE, I was dressing for a dance. I'd spent an hour ratting and spraying my hair into a big puff ball bouffant and was searching through one of my mother's drawers for a slip when my fingers encountered something hard beneath the silky lingerie. I lifted a folded nightgown. It was the doll's head.

What a strange place to keep it all those years, at the bottom of a drawer, gently padded with nightgowns, as if my mother had never decided what to do with it. Without touching it, I closed the drawer.

"I saw the doll's head when I was looking for that slip," I told my mother while she fixed dinner the next evening.

"Oh yes? It's been there for years." She smiled as if this were a fact that anyone should know. "Someday I'll do something with it. You remember how angry I was with you when you broke it?" She smiled again.

"How could I forget?"

Years later she did do something with it. She took it to a doll maker. He attached a new body. My mother told me that the body was not as fine a porcelain as the head.

The doll stood on the piano in my parents' living room. When my husband and I flew down from Maryland with our son and daughter to visit my parents in Texas, I saw the doll, but I never looked at it closely. From a distance, I imagined that the glass eyes stared out of the cold porcelain face and that the rosy cheeks appeared as artificial as the rouged cheeks of an old woman.

MY PARENTS DECIDED to visit and stay with our son and daughter for a weekend so my husband and I could go off on our own. We checked into an old hotel with potted palms, plush carpets, gilded mirrors, and quiet breakfasts in a wood paneled dining room.

The first night there I had my own nightmare. In it, my mother lay in a bed draped with white sheets. Her hair was gray and wispy, her body frail. I stood beside the bed, and she sat part way up, grasping my hand and wailing,

"They're going to take me to a concentration camp. They're going to take me to a camp. You won't be able to stop them. You can't stop them."

I screamed, "No they won't, Mom. Don't worry. I won't let anything happen to you. You're my mother. I won't let anything happen to you!"

That's when I woke up, fully awake right away—full of the determination I'd felt in my dream but none of the strength. I didn't want to confront her fears for the rest of my life.

MY MOTHER STOOD behind a lectern in my daughter's high school classroom. Students from two classes had crowded into the room. Every one of them stared up at her. She was talking about the reason for her escape, saying they had to leave without identity cards and passports because theirs were stamped *J* for *Jew*. She was beginning the story about her high school friend, Yette, who gave my mother her Dutch identity card with no *J* stamped on it because Yette was not Jewish.

"I asked my friend to meet me so I could tell her we were leaving. I knew I might never see her again.

"My friend reached into her pocket, pulled out her identity card, and pressed it into my hand. She would not hear my protests. She insisted that I take it."

I'd heard this story many times. Yette, only a year or two older than these students, was thrown into a Nazi prison in The Hague. My mother told me a Nazi soldier on the street asked Yette for her identity card and discovered she didn't have one.

But now, my mother was talking about the son of the farmer in the southern part of the Netherlands who let my mother, Moms, and Tante Nannie sleep in his house the first day of the escape. I'd never heard about the farmer's son before.

"I heard the farmer's son was taking the train to The Hague the next day. I asked him to find my friend and return her identity card. It was a big mistake."

My mother looked out at the students. They waited. Not moving in their seats. All eyes on her.

I stared at her, too—bewildered. This familiar story had begun to sound so different.

"I should not have asked him to do that," my mother said. "The Nazis checked everyone on his train for identity cards. The farmer's son was so scared, he showed them my friend's card. The Nazis arrested the farmer's son. They put him and my friend in a Nazi prison in The Hague.

"I shouldn't have asked him to return that identity card," my mother said to the classroom full of teenagers. "They both went to prison. I shouldn't have asked him."

The story about Yette's identity card had always made me wonder if I could risk my own safety to help another person. But now, stunned, I wondered, instead, how my mother could have lived with that guilt. Had she known ever since she'd contacted Yette after the war?

My mother had kept secret from me the real reason Yette was thrown into prison, and the farmer's son, too. Now, my mother was telling a group of teenagers—and telling me.

While my mother answered questions, I remembered when nearly ten years earlier she'd asked Israel to recognize Yette as one of the Righteous Among the Nations for risking herself to help save my mother. My mother had said very little to me about the ceremony held by the Israeli Ambassador in The Hague or about my parents' visit with Yette and her husband for several days afterward. Maybe it was during that visit Yette had told my mother about the farmer's son showing the Nazis the wrong identity card.

Today, my mother could have spoken to my daughter's class about any part of her escape. But she'd concentrated on this one part. It must have been the only way she could bear to tell me—with all those kids around us.

I wouldn't ask my mother when Yette had told her. I couldn't make her speak to me alone about it.

After hugging my daughter goodbye, my mother and I walked out of the classroom, down the hall past the art projects on the walls, into the glaring sun of the parking lot. I was driving her over to lunch at Tante Sonja's house where my mother would stay for the last few days of her visit.

I kept my eyes on the highway. "You're a good speaker," I said. "The kids were really listening."

But in my mind I heard, *I shouldn't have asked him. I shouldn't have asked him. They both went to prison.*

That afternoon, I took empty back roads home from Tante Sonja's house—and wept.

THE DOLL FOLLOWED MY PARENTS to assisted living. On the walls in that small room hung a Dutch tile picture of trees and windmills, a poster of the Sephardic synagogue in Amsterdam my mother often told me looked like her synagogue in The Hague, blue Chagall lovers, and my mother's own oil paintings of windmills, flowers, and trees. On what had formerly served as their dining room buffet—among a crystal bear and rabbit, a porcelain mother and child, a green and purple blown glass bowl, dozens of other knickknacks, and pictures of my wedding, my son's and daughter's graduations, my brother, my nephew, and assorted relatives—stood the doll. I never looked at it, though I often looked at the family pictures.

For a year and a half after Dad died, every night when I called my mother, and often in the daytime when someone from assisted living called me because she'd tried to escape, my mother was consumed with anxiety. She was sure that she needed to go somewhere with her sisters, but she didn't know how to buy the plane tickets, and she couldn't pack. I told her that she didn't need to leave, that her sisters didn't want to travel, that they wanted to stay at home like she did. She asked where they lived and where she lived, and when I answered her questions, she thanked me for telling her she could stay where she was, that she didn't need to be afraid, that she didn't need to run away with her sisters.

MY MOTHER LAY IN HER BED in assisted living. The room was filling with close family friends. My brother and I were carrying in chairs from the common area. People were talking and hugging each other and trying to communicate with my mother who occasionally opened her eyes. A friend who knew the doll was my mother's childhood toy told me it should be on the table beside her bed.

"You can put it there, if you want," I said.

I didn't see the doll even then, though I spent the day hugging and kissing my mother, holding her hands, and speaking to her in Dutch.

THE DAY BEFORE THE FUNERAL, my brother, my cousin, and I talked to the rabbi. He asked me about my mother's life in The Hague.

"They were in the upper middle class," I said. Then I couldn't speak. That was the moment I realized the mother whose life I'd lived—had died. I bowed my head so no one could see my face, closed my eyes and clenched all my muscles. I pointed at my cousin, Tante Sonja's son, born in Paramaribo one year before me. He told the rabbi about the grandfather we never met, about the movie theaters and the shoe store, and about the escape. When the feelings subsided enough for me to lift my head, my brother said, "I never heard any of these stories."

I looked at him. Fourteen years younger, he had heard none of the stories about the escape or about her life. She had poured it all into me and told him nothing.

That afternoon, packing up our mother's belongings, my brother and I agreed on general categories of items we'd each take. While he loaded the books onto a cart to take to his car, he picked up the doll and showed it to me.

"Really, Ingrid, you should have this. Don't you want it?"

"No."

"You should have it," he urged.

"I can't tell you how much I do not want that doll," I said. "Please take it."

He put it on the cart.

A YEAR LATER, I opened an email from the United States Holocaust Memorial Museum and found a picture of a survivor looking at a doll. The caption explained she had donated her doll to the Museum.

I emailed my brother and asked if we should try to give them the doll. I live near the Museum and could show it to them. He couldn't remember even having the doll but emailed back later that I would be receiving it by UPS the next day at 3:00 p.m.

The doll would be in my house the next day. I couldn't turn it away. I thought we would discuss the idea of donating it, or maybe it would take him a long time to find the doll and mail it. But almost instantly the doll was on its way to my house.

The atmosphere of my house would be tainted by the doll's presence. Even if I left it in the box and stuffed the box into a closet in the basement or up in the attic, I would know the doll was here.

The next day, at 10 in the morning, way too early, the UPS delivery woman stood at my front door holding a big white box. Dread coursed through my veins.

"Oh, no. It's here," I said.

The delivery woman looked at my face and blurted out, "Oh, I'm sorry! I'm so sorry!"

"It's not your fault," I assured her as I took the package. I wondered what she thought she was delivering.

I left the unopened box in the middle of the kitchen table. I would open it when I returned home that evening.

At the time I had appointed, I slit the packing tape, lifted the box flaps and pulled out several layers of bubble wrap.

There, tightly wrapped in a white towel, lay the doll. I reached into the box to pull the towel back from the doll's head. My hand shook. I held onto the towel's edge. I expected to see glassy eyes and a haughty masklike face. But as I slowly drew back the towel, the porcelain face looked soft, like a young child's, the eyelashes long, and the cheeks a light pink. This was the face that had entranced me when I was three years old. I leaned closer to cradle the head and lift the doll's towel swaddled body from the box. But instead—

I stared. Very clearly etched on either side of that beguiling childlike face was a long, thin crack.

The End

Afterword and Sources

THE DOLL IS CREATIVE NONFICTION. THE DIALOGUE AND SETTINGS are based on my memories of when my mother first told me her stories. I've included my genuine thoughts and reactions. The substance of my mother's story is based on my extensive interviews of my mother when her memories were quite tangible, the several talks I heard my mother deliver—including her interview at the United States Holocaust Memorial Museum—and the documents she left for me.

After her death, I discovered that my mother had saved a large collection of her escape documents for me. She'd told me for many years that I would one day need to look in a particular cabinet where she kept her financial records. When that day arrived, I found—all related to the escape—train tickets, ration cards, cards for hotels, a menu from the ship S.S. Nyassa, pictures of people and houses in Surinam, a postcard reporting that friends were still living, her lesson notebooks from Surinam, an official statement from the Dutch government-in-exile that my mother had completed her degree, her Dutch passport and other transit documents issued in Surinam, airline information for her flights from Surinam to D.C. I also found her resume.

In addition to the sources mentioned above, I also relied upon:

Lucy S. Dawidowicz, *The War Against the Jews 1933-1945*, 10th ed. (New York: Bantam Books, 1986).

Joods Historisch Museum Amsterdam, *Documents of the persecution of the Dutch Jewry 1940-1945*. Amsterdam: Atheneaum - Polak & Van Gennep, 1979. Exhibition catalogue.

Acknowledgements

My great appreciation to my friends and fellow writers who read parts of the manuscript and offered comments through the years as I wrote this book. Your support and thoughts were invaluable: Michelle Brafman, astute teacher, author, and leader of the Glen Echo Workshop for writers, Elinor Spieler, Ruth Catan, Myriam Delhij, Syma Ralston, William Schofield, David Kuhla, John Dix, Gregg Sangillo, Barbara Altman, Fran Parker, Jeffrey and Mindy Katz, and the writers in the Glen Echo Workshop. My deep gratitude to my friends, author Carol Solomon who read the entire manuscript and asked tough questions and author Janet Walenta who poured over *My Separate Worlds* and made important suggestions. Warm thanks to author Rona Simmons who has guided me through the book world.

CPSIA information can be obtained
at www.ICGtesting.com
Printed in the USA
LVHW051443160620
658144LV00010B/1335